DEMOCRACY ON TRIAL,
ALL RISE!

Democracy on Trial, All Rise!

Anuradha Kataria

Algora Publishing
New York

Library of Congress Cataloging-in-Publication Data —

Kataria, Anuradha, 1968-
  Democracy on trial, all rise! / Anuradha Kataria.
    p. cm.
  Includes bibliographical references and index.
    ISBN 978-0-87586-810-3 (soft cover: alk. paper) — ISBN 978-0-87586-811-0
(hard cover: alk. paper) — ISBN 978-0-87586-812-7 (ebook) 1. Democracy. 2. Political
participation. I. Title.
  JC423.K33 2010
  321.8—dc22
                        2010034722

Front cover: IMAGE: © Zahid Hussein/Reuters/Corbis

Printed in the United States

Democracy forever teases us with the contrast between its ideals and its realities, between its heroic possibilities and its sorry achievements.

—Agnes Repplier (American Essayist, 1855–1950)

TABLE OF CONTENTS

CHAPTER 1. DEMOCRACY AMIDST POVERTY: THE FORBIDDEN FRUIT

There are many ways of arriving at the truth. The ancient Greeks, for instance, considered contemplation to be the supreme mechanism. They believed in "ideal" theories based on logic or intuition, and if evidence from real life experiments contradicted that, then new theoretical constructs were added to explain away the problem. For instance, a circle was supposed to represent a theoretical ideal and perfect symmetry, and hence it was necessary that the planetary orbits be perfect circles. When observation conflicted with this idea, new cosmic bodies were invented to account for the distortion; but the perfect theory was not challenged, as senses were believed to be deceptive and not the true means of understanding the world. Ptolemy had back then made a systematic study of astronomy and refraction; but he did not arrive at the right laws because he used complicated mathematical models to explain deviations from his *a priori* theories.

This trend continued in a more subtle form in the Middle Ages as students studied texts, the Church upheld dogmas, and scientific enquiry was equated with heresy or black magic. The Scientific Revolution changed all that beginning around AD 1500. But in politics we are still following the earlier approach—even though we are not aware of it.

We have made detailed observations and studies of different nations' political and economic history but we view it all through the lens of *a priori* theories. That is the reason we are unable to explain why things don't work in the political world as we thought they would or insist they should. Democracy is analogous to the Greek obsession with a perfect circle—an ideal theory that should deliver an ideal world. But has it, or not, and why or why not?

The answer can be found by following the scientific approach which revolves around forming a hypothesis and then testing it. For nearly a century now, we have had the hypothesis that democracy is the ideal political model for all countries. This hypothesis has been tested amply in varying circumstances. We need to take stock and assess the results. The solution has to be derived from, not imposed on, real world experience. We may not like to challenge our theory, which we do quite love, as we loved our theory back when the Earth was thought to be at the center of the universe; but our delusion may be causing much harm and misery in the world.

The truth need not be feared; challenging democracy will not lead us to tyrannies, whereas not challenging actually might. The scientific investigation must begin, and here it does.

Mass democracy, where virtually all adults have a right to vote, is a 20th-century phenomenon. Most of the developed countries that have well-established democracies took a long time reaching this stage. Mostly, they started with an oligarchic form of it, where only the propertied white males had the right to vote. This was gradually extended to the entire adult population over the course of a century or two. Thus at the individual level, political empowerment followed economic empowerment. This was not a mere coincidence but a well thought-through strategy. It was then understood that a mass democracy of the largely poor (which these nations were, two to three centuries ago), would be unstable and subversive. This view was upheld by many thinkers of the Enlightenment Age and many of the early American founders as well as ancient Greek philosophers. Plato even implied that it is better to be ruled by a bad tyrant, since then there is only one person committing bad deeds, than by a bad democracy, since then all the people are responsible for such acts.[1]

More than two millennia down the line, that seems to ring true when we look at the tragic fate of democracy in many of the developing countries in Africa, Asia, etc. Democracy means "people power," but that does not mean that it cannot be abused. Power needs to be dealt with and a dominant pros-

---

1 Plato, *The Republic*, Book VI, VIII (360 B.C.E.), translated by Benjamin Jowett, The Internet Classics, http://classics.mit.edu/Plato/republic.html

perous middle class may be able to handle it well; but perhaps a largely destitute class cannot, as they easily allow it to be usurped by wrong elements. Further, in the decentralized form of governance that democracy is, a ticket to the parliament may become a means of cornering meager resources and easy power. The corrupt and the violent join politics at the grassroots in poor nations.

Regional dynamics have an important role to play in the political evolution of a country. Let us examine a few examples from different regions, starting with the most disastrous of all, Africa, moving on to the Middle East and then to India—often considered the best example of a successful democracy in the developing world. But to wrap it all up, we also will need to go back to the history of the developed nations like the United Kingdom and France to see when and how they got it right and when they got it wrong.

AFRICA

A great many African nations gained freedom from colonial rule around 1960 and started out with hopes and dreams of a glorious free era, with democracy. But what followed was bloodshed and violence unprecedented perhaps even in their long history of slavery or colonial rule and apartheid. What caused this violence and what are the political lessons from it—lessons that can lead us to solutions? Did African people fail at democracy or has democracy failed them?

The Democratic Republic of the Congo—the Most Violent Place on Planet Earth

It may come as a surprise to some that the most violent place on planet Earth is the Democratic Republic of the Congo, yet this has been so since about 1998 post the overthrow of a dictator in a quest for democracy. The civil war which then started has been proclaimed the deadliest conflict since World War II, with over 5 million[1] deaths in a nation with population of but 68 million. There are UN convoys who have visited Afghanistan, Iraq and Bosnia, but nothing quite prepares them for the level of hideous violence perpetrated against women and children in Congo. Brutal gang rapes of 4-month-old babies to 80-year-old women, mutilation of internal

---

1 Congo Crisis, International Rescue Committee (IRC), http://www.theirc.org/special-reports/congo-forgotten-crisis

organs, social shunning, and the lack of medical care or any form of justice is commonplace and worsening each day.[1] The perpetrators are not just the soldiers or militia but also common people in hordes.

Why then is Congo not always in the news?

If there is a hellhole on Earth, it is the Democratic Republic of Congo. Why is it not in the limelight, why isn't everyone thinking and talking about it?[2] Maybe because we don't know whom to blame! It is always easier when a dictator is in the seat of power, like in Zimbabwe or Sudan, as we can lay the entire blame on him. We also have the quick fix solution—bring in democracy and all the problems will solve themselves. But we already condoned the overthrow of a dictator in Congo and nearly a decade after that (2006), democracy too has been ushered in. Yet violence has only escalated and no solution seems to be in sight.

To find a solution, we need to first understand—how did it get to be this way?

Congo gained independence from Belgian rule in 1960 and became a democratic republic. It soon descended into ethnic infighting and political violence. A coup brought Mobutu Sese Seko to power in 1965 and he ruled the nation for 32 years. He initially had the Western world's support due to his anti communist stand. He amassed personal wealth and wasn't a great leader but the nation still enjoyed good law and order under him. He failed to develop the nation or modernize the economy which remained dependent on agriculture and mining. This led to an economic crisis in the 1980s and internal pressure for reforms mounted. With the fall of communism in Russia and Eastern Europe by 1990, he was no longer needed as an ally and he soon lost Western support. In 1994, the nation's eastern borders faced a refugee crisis from the Rwandan civil war but violence was kept under check. Seeing his weak hand, Laurent-Désiré Kabila led a rebel movement to overthrow Mobutu, with help from Rwanda and Uganda. In 1997, Mobutu fled the nation and Kabila established a democratic republic and promised elections (which were not held). Within a year, civil war started as Kabila's relations with Uganda and Rwanda soured and new rebel movements were started for control of Congo, with help from these neighbor-

1 Between a rock and a hard place — Abuses in Congo, Ledio Cakaj, Enough, The project to end genocide and crimes against humanity, 11 Mar 2010, http://www.enoughproject.org/publications/lra-army-abuses-congo?page=show
2 "Orphaned, Raped and Ignored", Nicholas D Kristof, *The New York Times*, 30 Jan 2010, http://www.nytimes.com/2010/01/31/opinion/31kristof.html?_r=2

ing nations to the East. In the war-affected eastern region, civilians fled the areas where their families had lived for centuries, to refugee camps or to interior jungles where they lived like animals—without clothes or shelter, surviving on pickings. Most of the 5 million deaths so far have not been the result of firepower but of easily preventable diseases and starvation.

In 2001, Laurent Kabila was assassinated and his son, the 31-year-old Joseph Kabila, became president. Relatively unknown thus far, Joseph Kabila started negotiations with rebel leaders for peace and the civil war was officially declared over in 2003. However, as per the International Rescue Committee (IRC), the mortality rate remained unchanged at 45,000 deaths per month, even post this declaration. The civil war had not ended.

In 2005, a referendum was held for the newly drafted constitution and elections were held in 2006; Kabila won. The National Assembly held its first session in September 2006. After this, especially after 2008, violence escalated. An Oxfam study[1] made some chilling observations claiming rape had risen 17-fold and 38% rapes were committed by civilians in 2008 compared with less than 1% in 2004. Of those assaults 56% were in the victim's house in the presence of her family, including children. The AIDS epidemic too increased sharply. While violence in eastern and northern bordering areas was going up, a separate conflict started in the previously peaceful western province of Equateur in 2009. The nation also continues to teeter on the edge of bankruptcy, with the IMF and the World Bank often intervening. It has the lowest per capita income in the world. In retrospect, Mobutu Sese Seko did not develop the country as expected—but he only led it to stagnation, not complete ruin. That came only with the ethnically-inspired power struggles between different rebel factions after he was overthrown to establish a democratic republic. Further, the 2000s saw the rise of a weak leader, Joseph Kabila, whose only claim to the "throne" was being the son of Laurent Kabila. He was unable to control the violence. And that got even worse after the turn to democracy in 2006. Already in a calamitous state, from 2008 onwards atrocities have surged in scale and degree of brutality[2]. While large rebel groups exist, tiny gangs of thugs calling themselves rebels have mushroomed all over the country. All of them exploit the

1 Congo Report Shows Rape is Widespread — Oxfam report, Amy Fallon, guardian.co.uk, 15 Apr 2010, http://www.guardian.co.uk/world/2010/apr/15/congo-rape-widespread-oxfam-report

2 Violence in Congo Worsens, Simon Tisdall, guardian.co.uk, 10 Apr 2009, http://www.guardian.co.uk/world/2009/apr/10/congo-united-nations-aid

natural resources to buy weapons, and using that power, murder and rape people at will. Incredibly, the era of Belgian colonial rule is viewed with nostalgia[1] as the people at least lived peacefully.

As per UN reports, the government troops are involved in the worst forms of violence, especially sexual violence. The common people themselves engage in widespread crime and brutalities against each other. Even the UN troops hailing from India, Bangladesh and Egypt allegedly have been involved in gold and arms trafficking. This seems a textbook example to prove Plato's theory that a bad tyrant is far better than a bad democracy, as under the former only one person is responsible for bad deeds whereas under the latter all the people are now responsible for such deeds.

Congo has descended into lawlessness and is on a suicidal path. Already suffering from weak leadership, the nation has suffered even more in the wake of democratic reforms that seem to have further weakened the state authority. The assembly and legislature are merely paper-pushing entities meant to keep the international forces happy but having no relevance or meaning in reality. Congo is without hope on the current path.

Nigeria—Poor and Divided

Despite being an oil-rich nation, about 64% of Nigeria's population lives below the poverty line[2]. The nation has had a checkered past since its independence from British colonial rule in 1960, with weak fractious democracies alternating with military rules. The main problem since its inception has been the conflict between its three separate regions, the predominantly Muslim North, Christian East and the mixed West. The regions are also split along ethnic lines, as historically they were never united. Pre- and post-independence politics remained divided along these lines, leading to regional and ethnic violence. As in DR Congo, in Nigeria too, the initial 5–6 years of violent, fractious and increasingly chaotic democratic rule led the military to stage a coup in 1966. A civil war started as the North and West tried to exclude the East from sharing in the oil revenues. The Eastern Igbos sought secession but this revolt was soon quelled by the military.

---

1 "Dinner with a Warlord," Nicholas D Kristof, *The New York Times*, 18 Jun 2007, http://query.nytimes.com/gst/fullpage.html?res=9A02E7DC123FF93BA25755C0A 9619C8B63

2 Poverty line as per the World Bank revised definition of less than $1.25 a day, in Purchasing power parity terms. Human Development Report, 2009, UNDP

The following decade was relatively peaceful as the military rule helped ease regional tensions and reintegrated the Igbos back into the nation, remarkably smoothly, and established law and order. Some of the oil wealth was ploughed back into the nation and development-oriented reforms were initiated. The last military ruler, Olusegun Obasanjo, ushered in democracy voluntarily in 1979, following a constitutional amendment to dissolve and defuse regionalization of politics. This required the president and the vice president to win not only in the overall elections but also to secure at least 25% votes in two thirds of the states. This was to force parties to widen their appeal beyond their regional ethnic vote blocs.

But the democratic phase did not last long as it was riddled with government corruption, economic mismanagement and, in 1983, rigged elections. A series of coups and counter coups followed as the nation returned to military rule. After several attempts, democracy was once again restored in 1999 and its progressive military leader of the late 1970s, Obasanjo, returned as the elected head. As proven during his military rule too, he was a secularist who believed in uniting Nigerians and was also a leader who respected the constitution. However, the first few years of this democracy were plagued by communal violence across the country, instigated by local politicians who paid youth to ignite ethnic and religious violence[1] either in the run up to elections or post elections to dispute results. Many large scale riots occurred in the northern and middle states during 2000 and 2001, leading to thousands of deaths. In 2001, Obasanjo constituted a National Security Commission to address communal violence issues. Being a powerful and effective leader, he brought down large scale riots but violent clashes spurred by local politicians continued. Crime also crept into the oil rich Niger delta as kidnappings, extortions and killings became commonplace. Here too, self styled militants colluded with local politicians and military officers to steal oil and sell it in the black market[2].

Clashes between religious and ethnic groups often spawned by local political disputes have killed thousands of Nigerians since 1999, when democracy returned. It is noteworthy here that under the same leader, this did not happen when he ruled as a military head in the 1970s. The issue here is the contrast between a strong central leadership, as under a military rule,

---

1 "Religious violence rages in Nigeria," Will Connors, *Time*, 5 Dec 2008, http://www.time.com/time/world/article/0,8599,1864801,00.html

2 Nigeria's oil violence, BBC News, 5 Oct 2006, http://news.bbc.co.uk/2/hi/africa/5409488.stm

versus decentralized power in a democracy where local political groups in nexus with criminals hold much more sway. In 2007, Obasanjo stepped aside as per the constitutional bar on third terms, but he has remained an influential figure. Under his rule and continued influence, the nation gained some semblance of stability. But poverty, corruption and violence continue to define life for an average Nigerian. The world is under the mistaken notion that democracy is on a precarious path in Nigeria; perhaps it is democracy that has put Nigeria on a precarious path.

Kenya—Riches to Rags

Despite the fact that it is a divided country with about 40 ethnic tribes, Kenya did quite well for more than two decades after independence in 1963. The reason was its first leader, Jomo Kenyatta, who was also a national hero during Kenya's struggle for freedom. He won the initial election but decided to suspend democracy soon after and ruled Kenya for about 15 years till his death. A secularist, Kenyatta appointed members of many different ethnic groups to government positions. He encouraged Kenyans to come together as one rather than focus on their different ethnic alignments. In addition to enforcing unity and stability, the economy was also managed well. Export crops like coffee and tea were encouraged and friendly relations with the West ensured foreign investment as well as markets for Kenyan exports. Kenyatta's secular ideals were continued post his death by Daniel arap Moi who also tried to limit the corrupt divisive tactics of local political leaders. President Moi made it plain that the party branches were not to be operated as special clubs for ambitious local leaders but as a means for the mass involvement of people in the political life of the country.

However, the Kenyan economy slowed down in the 1980s due to cyclical droughts. Under international as well as domestic pressure, politics was opened up in 1991–92, ushering in multi party democracy with regular elections. What was the impact of this development? First and foremost, the parties split along ethnic lines and communal violence started creeping in, especially in the election years. This was usually instigated by political rivals to develop ethnic vote blocs. Moi was the first leader who said that violence in Africa was not on account of tribalism but multi party democracy.[1] But Moi and the continued KANU party's dominance were long seen

---

1 Kenya: Barely Escaping Rwanda, President Moi's argument that multi-party democracy not tribalism is the cause of violence, Bill Berkeley, 1995, http://www.

as the reason for Kenya's problems. In 2002, his rule finally came to an end, which was welcomed as a relief. The new Kenyan president was invited to "Washington" to celebrate the dawn of a new era when Kenya was finally free to pursue multiparty democracy.[1]

But Moi's prediction was to come true, as Kenya was rocked by severe electoral violence[2] among its ethnic groups post the 2007 elections. The reason was that in the contested election abundant rigging happened by both the dominant parties, yet the loser cried foul and instigated mob violence. Brutalities grabbed international headlines and once again "tribalism" was propped up as the reason for the violence. However, some journalists like Mark Doyle of BBC deciphered the situation better as "Tribal differences in Kenya, normally accepted peacefully, are exploited by politicians hungry for power who can manipulate poverty-stricken population"[3]. Finally, a truce has been made between rival parties with a coalition government in place. But come the next round in 2012, there is every chance that history will repeat itself with contested elections and riots. Summing up, ethnically diverse Kenya was united and peaceful under the long secularist rule of the KANU party but a turn to multiparty democracy brought communal violence. We could still blame the Kenyan people and their political representatives for not understanding democracy well enough. But does that not indicate that they are not ready for decentralized democracy?

The important issue is not who is to blame but to establish systems that work in reality, such that there is no need to blame. On the current path, Kenya might just witness the ever increasing spiral of violence and partisanship that has become the hallmark of democracy in Africa.

South Africa—What Went Wrong?

Let us go back to the 1990s, when years of injustice and oppression were about to end and all eyes were on the horizon for a glorious new dawn to

aliciapatterson.org/APF1701/Berkeley/Berkeley.html

1 "Kenya After Moi," Joel D Barkan, Jan-Feb 2004, *Foreign Affairs*, http://www.foreignaffairs.com/articles/59535/joel-d-barkan/kenya-after-moi

2 "Fear and Loathing in Nairobi," John Githongo, Jul/Aug 2010, *Foreign Affairs*, http://www.foreignaffairs.com/articles/66470/john-githongo/fear-and-loathing-in-nairobi. The two articles from the same source should be read in that order to see how we first theorize that democracy will now transform this nation and soon recoil in horror as it does transform but for the worse.

3 Kenya Stokes Tribalism Debate, Mark Doyle, 4 Jan 2008, BBC News, http://news.bbc.co.uk/2/hi/africa/7168551.stm

break. The end to apartheid and turn to popular democracy was one of the longest and hardest fought struggles in the world. Taking a whole nation's dream with him, Nelson Mandela won the first truly democratic elections in 1994 with a thumping majority and roaring applause from rest of the world. The revolution did not lack in perspiration either; the constitution was debated at length, drawn and redrawn several times, challenged by the constitutional court; it finally went into effect in 1997. It included a comprehensive bill of rights, was the first in Africa to allow same-sex marriages and the first in the world to prohibit discrimination based on sexual orientation. Mandela was succeeded by Thabo Mbeki and the elections in South Africa remained "free and fair" as adjudged by international bodies.

The impact this new political empowerment had on the nation is however a sorry tale which seems to turn more tragic as time goes by. The poor nation with vast inequalities in income, education, and the ever divisive color, was not able to handle the sudden opening up. Violence increased alarmingly, and crime became rampant, adding up to near total anarchy in the society. The violence has little to do with color anymore; it is widespread and all encompassing with even surprising xenophobic turns against African immigrants from countries with whose support South Africa originally won its independence. Elaborate theories have been concocted to explain this phenomenon, even suggesting "violence seems almost genetic to Africa."

But isn't this the common fate of democracy in the developing world and doesn't it have less to do with Africa, its people or its leaders than with the circumstances in which they found themselves? The old power structure was destroyed, and needless to say, it had to be. But it has been replaced by decentralized politics with power in the hands of local thugs ruling over the hopeless and desperate poor. Law and order has broken down and South Africa today is considered the crime capital of the world. About 20% of the adult population is suffering from AIDS but there is widespread ignorance about the disease. Rape has risen to an alarming level, and regressive patriarchal values have become stronger.

South Africa needs to fix its chronic problems by investing in education, healthcare, combating AIDS, etc. Instead it seems embroiled in a cycle of increasing violence, corruption and general anarchy. To make matters worse, now a leader like Jacob Zuma has become the president. He has brought an ethnic angle to the political game, appears to be obtusely ignorant about

AIDS, has battled rape charges himself and in general advocates patriarchal social norms and culture. This has added to his popularity among the largely regressive and poor majority. Democracy is but the voice of a nation's majority. Now South Africa is being deformed from both ends—at the grassroots by criminal warlords and at the center by a leader who is fast becoming the epitome of precisely those things that South Africa needs to change. Needless to say, democracy has not delivered justice, equality, peace or prosperity thus far, and worse still, does not seem to be even going in that direction. ANC and progressive leaders in an empowered form of political model are perhaps the answer to the nation's problems. But decentralized and regressive democracy raises a question mark on the nation's future.

We will return to examine some of these nations, especially South Africa as well as the Rwandan genocide, later under "Fundamentalism." For the moment let us turn our attention to the better-off nations in Africa.

Others—The Ones that Got Away

The better developed nations in Africa are along the northern Mediterranean coast like Libya, Tunisia, Algeria, Egypt and Morocco. Most of these Islam dominant nations have not attempted democracy and their respective rulers have uniformly resisted the rise of fundamentalism. They have made concerted efforts in secularizing education and also supported women's rights by resisting *Sharia* law, often demanded by the populace. Algeria experimented with democracy but has since struggled with Islamic fundamentalism and public support thereof. In most of the rest, a stable central rule and secular ideals seem to have worked. It is not that ethnic divisions do not exist here; for example Libya has had a long history of provincial differences between Tripolitania and Cyrenaica. But democracy has never gotten a chance to ignite this divide; thus the nation has been spared violence and animosity. This is not to say that civil wars never happen under other regimes, a very obvious case in point being Sudan, which was first racked by a North–South Civil war and then Darfur. But the incidence of civil wars and violence seems almost a certainty under democracy of the poor, whereas it is only a feeble probability under other systems.

Democracy has failed spectacularly in most African nations, often leading to long term fractures and tragic humanitarian crises. It does not look like the way forward at all. Africa does not lack in true leaders or resources. It lacks stability and a different and more reasonable political model better suited to its socioeconomic context. We have to find that solution, or allow Africa to do so, but we cannot go on promoting inherently violent and divisive democracy and, when faced with failure, add insult to injury by blaming it on the people's lack of social qualities and so forth. If they do not understand democracy, as has often been said, then democracy is the wrong model in the first place. Africa has not failed democracy; it is democracy that is failing Africa.

Let us look at other developing regions to see how democracy has fared there.

THE MIDDLE EAST

Despite having abundant precious resources like the coveted oil, many nations in the Middle East struggle with uneven development as well as poverty. Peace and progress eludes them and in turn the world through terrorism and oil price fluctuations. We still believe democracy is the answer to these problems. At some point the question must be answered that apart from it being a theoretical ideal like a circle, why is democracy an answer to the developing world's problems? What evidence from the real world supports that theory? Or is it a conclusion so absolute that we don't need or care to prove it? Let us look at two contrasting examples from this region, Iraq, that was pushed into a democracy, and Iran, which established a form of demo-theocracy through a people's revolution. Nevertheless the result in terms of a shift towards fundamentalism has been a common denominator in both.

Iraq—Uphill Democracy

Before the US-led invasion in 2003, Iraq was ruled by an autocratic leader who allowed little political freedom and mercilessly crushed rebel movements. But Iraqi women enjoyed considerable freedom and had rights by constitution[1] that were among the broadest in any Arab or Islamic nation. Iraq upheld secular values and despite the Gulf wars, there was law and order in the state—all this under a so-called "barbaric" dictator. That the US-led war itself could have been avoided is already an oft-repeated

---

[1] Iraqi Women under Saddam, Marjorie P Lasky, A report by Codepink, Women for peace and global exchange, 24 Apr 2006, http://www.alterinter.org/article170.html?lang=fr

story. Even if misinformation led to it, when weapons of mass destruction were not found, an apology and a quick exit with perhaps some reparations to Iraq could still have saved the day. But pursuit of the elusive mirage called democracy has been the undoing of both the nations—the victimized as well as the victimizer. Iraq has descended into turmoil but the US, the perpetrator, too has suffered casualties, economic damage and the entire world's ire on account of it. What has democracy indeed brought to Iraq?

The political landscape has been split along its three factions—the Shias, the Arab Sunnis and the Kurds, and also certain sub sects within each. Each of them has tried to corner the oil wealth and exclude the others. The result is a complete breakdown of law and order. Women have lost all their rights and are at the mercy of self-styled vigilantes. Even the laws as per the new constitution are more regressive[1] for women than they were under Saddam. Thus the "democracy" established in 2005 became a proxy front for sectarian wars, and violence escalated out of control. Casualties estimates are unclear with varying reports ranging from 0.1 million to 1 million deaths and about 4.5 million refugees or internally displaced people. As is common in war-torn regions, a majority of children are suffering from trauma-related symptoms and mental disorders.

Since 2009, the local Iraqi leadership gained some foothold and with the strengthening of Iraqi security forces, violence came down a little. However, even months after the March 2010 elections, Iraq's divergent splintered factions are yet to agree on a coalition government.[2] There is no need to blame Iraq's leaders or its people for how they handled democracy—they neither asked for nor were ready for it; it was just thrust upon them violently and arbitrarily. It is still not clear what the goal of this war was, after all. However as the US pulls out its troops as planned, the post election inability to form a coalition government has already led to a rise in violence and Iraq seems to be going back in time again. Can Iraq progress and achieve lasting peace with its current fractious democracy?

---

1 Women miss Saddam, Abdu Rahman and Dahr Jamail, IPS News, Baghdad, 2010, http://ipsnews.net/news.asp?idnews=50642

2 "No government in sight in Iraq," Salah Hemeid, *Al-Ahram Weekly*, 17-23 Jun 2010, http://weekly.ahram.org.eg/2010/1003/re7.htm

Iran—Disputed Democracy

In contrast to Iraq, in Iran a people's movement overthrew its stable Shah monarchy in 1979 through the Islamic revolution. Iranians voted over-whelmingly in a referendum[1] on 1 April 1979 to establish an Islamic republic. Whereas the Shah had modernized Iran, worked on women's emancipa-tion, focused on scientific, secular education and economic development, the people's revolution led to a sharp reversal of these policies. Let us briefly assess the journey of this regime since then. Right after the revolution, the nation was plunged into a war with Iraq. The end of this war coincided with Iran's religious leader Khomeini passing away in 1989. The 1990s brought some progressive politics in Iran as President Rafsanjani assumed power and proved to be a pragmatic leader. He focused on rebuilding the war-ravaged economy and infrastructure.[2] Later, he also lent his support to moderate reformers like Khatami who championed greater civil liberties and tolerance. In the late 1990s, Khatami became the president and the re-formers[3] also later won a majority in the parliament. But many of their bills were banned by the clergy, plus this government was a coalition of a large number of parties which deliberated much and achieved little, as is the case with most large coalitions.

Beginning about 2004, Iran's demo-theocracy took a downward turn, first with the clergy's ban on most of the liberal candidates, voter apathy to elections, and then the rise of Mahmoud Ahmadinejad who won with the support of conservatives and the clergy. In line with Supreme Leader Khamenei's ideology, Ahmadinejad stepped up the anti-US and anti-Israel rhetoric. While he had been little known thus far, this defiance catapulted him to a hero-like status not only within Iran but across the Middle East.[4] His support base was Iran's relatively poor and rural conservative majority as he also traveled in rural Iran extensively. Iran's economy meanwhile con-

---

1 Iran Archives, The Islamic Dream, BBC Panorama, http://news.bbc.co.uk/pan-orama/hi/front_page/newsid_8084000/8084881.stm
2 History of Modern Iran, Mid East Web, http://www.mideastweb.org/iranhistory.htm
3 By Popular Demand: Iranian Elections, 1997–2001, Frontline, http://www.pbs.org/wgbh/pages/frontline/shows/tehran/inside/elections.html
4 "Arabs See a Hero in Iran Leader," Jeffrey Fleishman, 24 Sept 2007, *Los Angeles Times*, http://articles.latimes.com/2007/sep/24/world/fg-ahmadinejad24

tinued to suffer and it started featuring among the highest inflation[1] econo-mies in the world. Yet Ahmadinejad won the 2009 elections in a landslide victory. This was followed by huge protests and outpouring as the election results were contested and widespread reports emerged of the arrested pro-testers being tortured in jails.[2] All the same, some evidence[3] has emerged of electoral pre polls suggesting Ahmadinejad's win may have been genuine. As we shall see later under "Wooing the Voters," radical and defiant strate-gies often work wonders with the voters.

Further, while much ado has been made internally and internation-ally about the 2009 elections, in essence what powers does the "elected" president possess? As per the Iranian constitution, the supreme religious leader has wide ranging powers.[4] He is the head of armed forces and has the sole power to declare war or peace. He appoints the heads of judiciary, state media, and police. He also has the final say on the foreign policy. The presidential or parliamentary candidates require his approval for election. Further, he can veto any or all of presidential and parliamentary decisions. Thereby, significant powers—legislative, executive, judiciary as well as spiritual, seem to rest with the supreme leader. Yet the elected authority is Ahmadinejad, so that a complex equation of power struggles has resulted in speculative reporting of goings-on, in the opaque scenario that exists with limited press freedom.

SOUTH ASIA

This region has some examples of relatively stable democracies, but gen-uine peace and progress eludes most of them too. Pakistan and Bangladesh followed a somewhat similar course with democratic regimes regularly al-

---

1 Top Five Countries with the Highest Inflation Rate, Aneki.com — Rankings + Records, Inflation Rates 2010 Countries by Rank, Countries of the World, http://www.photius.com/rankings/economy/inflation_rate_2010_0.html

2 'Torture, Murder and Rape' — Iran's Way of Breaking the Opposition, Martin Fletcher, 18 Sept 2009, *The Sunday Times*, http://www.timesonline.co.uk/tol/news/world/middle_east/article6839335.ece. Karroubi Takes on his Critics, 19 Aug 2009, Frontline — Tehran Bureau, http://www.pbs.org/wgbh/pages/frontline/tehranbureau/2009/08/karroubi-takes-on-his-critics.html

3 "The Iranian People Speak," Ken Ballen and Patrick Doherty, *The Washington Post*, 15 Jun 2009, http://www.washingtonpost.com/wp-dyn/content/article/2009/06/14/AR2009061401757.html

4 Leadership in the Constitution of the Islamic Republic of Iran, Article 110, The Of-fice of the Supreme Leader, http://www.leader.ir/langs/en/index.php?p=leader_law

ternating with military dictatorships. Sri Lanka has just ended a civil war that raged for three decades. Nepal, a monarchy for a long time, turned to democracy through a revolution and has already descended into anarchy, insurgent violence and factional fighting. In the East, Thailand and the Philippines too remain mired in politically instigated violence. The country-wise analysis could go on with ample examples from Asia where democracy has not moved nations forward but often turned them backwards. The military has many times stepped in to rescue these nations from chaos, corruption and lawlessness. But we need to move away from the rant of these failed democracies and take a turn in the direction which will most help clarify what exactly the problem with democracy is when it is brought amidst widespread poverty. Let us take a look at the Indian democracy.

India—A Nation in Denial

Large, populous and poor, the diverse nation was the least likely of places for democracy to succeed and yet India has remained stable and under civilian rule since its independence in 1947.

But just because democracy is stable in India does not mean that good governance is in place or even that the nation is on a progressive path. With 41.6% of population[1] estimated to be below poverty line, as compared to the world average of 26%, the world's largest number of poor live in India, given also its huge population base. Literacy[2] hovers at just about 66%, well below the world average of 84%. Female literacy is even lower, gender discrimination rampant, and heinous acts like dowry deaths have gone up considerably since independence. Some 72% of the population is rural and development remains concentrated around the few metropolitan areas and towns which have grown more and more congested with time. Even today, a low caste segment of *dalits*, about 100–150 million people, suffer an oppressive form of physical, social and emotional apartheid unparalleled even in colonial Africa. This is predominantly in rural India, where infrastructure, employment opportunities as well as law and order remains minimal.

Paradoxically, India also has a large base of urban, highly qualified people who have played an important role in India's presence in the global economy. This was on account of its first Prime Minister, Jawahar Lal

---

1 More people living below poverty line — The World Bank, Lesley Wroughton, Reuters, 26 Aug 2008, http://www.reuters.com/article/idUSN26384266

2 Literacy rates as per United Nations Development Program Report, 2009

Nehru, who believed institutions of higher learning ought to be developed alongside primary education. For a long time post independence, Indian politics was dominated by the Congress Party (which was initially led by Nehru and thereafter largely by members of his family). This proved crucial to keeping India together despite the centrifugal forces of diversity. Another factor that played a role in the stability was India's federal structure where divergent states were given sufficient autonomy. Traditionally, India has been a pluralistic and tolerant society. But post political opening up, India has faced a record number of separatist movements and its divides along language, religion, caste and regions have sharpened under democracy.

India has been stable and under continuous civilian rule, but corruption and violence at the grassroots, divisive politics and rising crime are just as endemic here as in any other developing country. While long used to peacefully living amidst diversity, now socially it is facing heightened tensions between different caste, religious, linguistic and regional factions. The reason, ironically, is democracy itself. Democracy politics opens up a form of opportunism for petty power mongers and even criminals[1] at the grassroots as one sure way to develop vote blocs is to instigate hatred and deepen the sectarian divides. The same is less true of the national level political leaders and they are the ones still holding it all together. But as the regional forces are becoming more dominant, given the recent electoral trend,[2] Indian stability and progressiveness is under threat.

If one strategy for maintaining Indian democracy is "divide and rule," then the other is "freebies," whereby political parties just empty the exchequer to distribute free commodities, color TVs, electrical power etc. in order to win voters. In the process, long-term investments like in infrastructure and education remain neglected. These investments require a long-term commitment, yet they bear fruit slowly and the populace views such development with suspicion, dismissing it as pro-rich. As a result, filth and squalor in urban India have risen to crisis levels. Drainage and water supply pipes are often mixed. Drinking water is contaminated with life-

---

1 "Criminals in Politics, B.G. Verghese, India — the Tasks Ahead," *The Tribune*, 2005, http://www.tribuneindia.com/2005/specials/tribune_125/main7.htm

2 "India's 2009 Elections : The Resilience of Regionalism and Ethnicity," Christophe Jaffrelot and Gilles Verniers, *South Asia Multidisciplinary Academic Journal*, SAMAJ, http://samaj.revues.org/index2787.html

threatening bacterial strains.[1] Cities are overcrowded, with pathetic roads, poor public transport, traffic congestion, power outages, and a lack of public parks, footpaths and even more basic requirements like access to clean toilets. Slums abound and are ghettos of misery, filth and crime. Ground water is fast being depleted[2] in India, threatening availability for drinking as well as agriculture, but the population explosion and wasteful agricultural practices continue.

India has made a mark on the world stage with its capitalization of low cost services especially in the IT area; that is commendable but the economic progress is ill matched by other development parameters. While it is still more stable and peaceful than any other developing world democracy, lawlessness is on the rise in India as well. One of the key reasons for that is the lack of an appropriate justice system. It requires considerable influence to get even a police complaint registered and there is an underlying police–criminal nexus anyway on account of criminalization of politics. Further, the legal system is in shambles. Cases take an average of ten to twenty years to come to any form of verdict while those who are indicted languish in jails, and the victims, too, go through emotional and financial bankruptcy while pressing their cases for so long.

The main problem is not just that these issues of social regression, crumbling infrastructure and deteriorating law and order plague the nation, but that there is a kind of denial of this stark reality, both within the country and without. The key reason for that is that the presence of democracy in India makes it a Western favorite and leads to a tendency to overlook all ills. The nation too gets carried away in the "at least we have democracy" illusion. For instance, there is much talk about its economic boom but the numbers tell a different tale. Of the four big emerging economies, Brazil, Russia, India and China, often called "BRIC," India is the smallest in terms of per capita income. Even in terms of absolute size, with its GDP[3] at $1.3 trillion, India is just marginally ahead of Russia at $1.2 trillion but behind Brazil at $1.5 trillion. They should ideally be reclassified as BRI and C, be-

---

1 "Human Waste Overwhelms India's war on disease," Kenneth J. Cooper, *Washington Post Foreign Service*, 17 Feb 1997, http://www.swopnet.com/engr/sanitation/India_sewers.html
2 Troubled Waters, Development Alternatives (DA), Water Management initiative in Urban and rural India, http://www.devalt.org/water/WaterinIndia/issues.htm
3 GDP (nominal) estimates as per World Bank, 2009 report

cause the Chinese economy, at \$4.9 trillion, is bigger than the other three put together and is growing faster besides.

It begs asking why India, globally a far more integrated country than China and with a large English-speaking population, lags far behind on all development parameters. China is easily 3–4 times the size of the Indian economy, has invested heavily in infrastructure, education and basic health care, reduced the proportion of its population below the poverty line, and as well has established good law and order. If democracy is the right model for a developing nation and unitary state the wrong one, then the theorists have some explaining to do as far as the anomaly of the India–China comparison. It is not coincidence and we must not forever dodge such difficult questions.

Democracy has succeeded in India but is it, maybe, failing the nation? Has it delivered good governance? No. India as a country needs to arrest its downward regression, socially and politically and to do that, it must no more be in denial of its reality. There is a lot of euphoria around GDP growth and India's participation in the knowledge economy. Those are clearly good planks to build on. However, thus far, the scope of India's achievements remains mediocre in terms of meeting the development needs of its large population base.

The course of myriad other developing countries since their independence is an all too familiar story of short-lived democracies interspersed with coups or worse still, civil wars. It would be good to turn our attention to Europe now to understand this issue better.

WESTERN EUROPE

Today most Western European nations are well developed with deeply entrenched democratic traditions. But they were like the developing world of today, just two or three centuries back. How and why did they make democracy work for them? What did they get right—or did they also maybe get it wrong sometimes? Let us examine.

The United Kingdom—The Pioneer

The UK, especially England, has played a pioneering role in the development of modern democracy, laying its foundation way back in 1215 with the introduction of Magna Carta. The charter was the first real step in the direction of "rule of law" as it checked the king's powers by demanding that his will be bound by law and that he protect certain rights of the subjects, such as the writ of habeas corpus. Although the charter was in force only for a short while, it was revived repeatedly throughout English history. After the Glorious Revolution of 1688, the government started functioning as per an unwritten constitution,[1] which remains unwritten to this date.

The power balance started to tip in favor of the parliament over the monarch. At that time, the rural poor formed the majority but voting rights were limited to a small minority of propertied males. It remained that way through the 18th century, towards the end of which Britain started industrializing following the "free markets" model. This led to the emergence of a new class, the middle class, which earned its living in the professions and trade and brought a focus on values, thrift and education.[2] As prosperity spread, suffrage or the right to vote was gradually extended, starting with the Reform Bill of 1832 which led to a decrease in the amount of land one had to own to qualify to vote. Still only 20% adult males now had the right to vote in England, 12% in Scotland and a mere 5% in Ireland. About 35 years later, the Reform Bill of 1867 doubled the male electorate and another 17 years later, the Reform Bill of 1884 tripled it. In 1918 all men over age 21 and women over age 30 (with some property restrictions), received the right to vote. It was not until 1928 that a gender-equal universal suffrage was finally achieved in the UK.

This seems like a rather long journey spread over centuries, and clearly economic empowerment was taking the lead with political empowerment following suit. This had certain drawbacks in that it kept the society divided along class lines, but it was inherently stable. Unlike the subversion of power in the hands of the landed aristocracy and nobility, the middle class handled it well and also produced leaders that championed the rights of the downtrodden. In 1807 and 1833, the British parliament passed laws to ban slavery within its empire and also enacted factory laws to regulate child labor around the same time. But industrialization and development are tricky processes. The metamorphosis that a society goes through in transitioning from a largely poor one to a middle-class-dominant society is not without its pains. The absence of democracy in the UK as well as

1 The UK Constitution, Nicola, McEwen, BBC News, 1 Sept 2003, http://news.bbc. co.uk/2/hi/programmes/bbc_parliament/2561719.stm
2 History of the United Kingdom, Mark Kishlansky, Microsoft® Encarta® Online Encyclopedia 2009

in other nations like the US arguably helped them go through their birth pangs and growing pains with a minimum of social revolt. The end result, however, has been political stability as well as overall high living standards compared to other nations.

Besides, prior to the establishment of democracy, Europe had been through a process of "opening up." The Renaissance, the Scientific Revolution, and the Age of Enlightenment prepared the society for decentralized power in the hands of people's representatives.

Why are the developing countries expected to skip all that, taking a straight and simple short cut to the end, in the hope that somehow it will work? It can't possibly. It didn't, even in Europe. The French Revolution is a controversial example which has enjoyed much glory in the annals but equally has received its share of criticism. The view here is consonant with the latter, albeit with different arguments and conclusions.

The French Revolution—A Mirage

One of the most acclaimed revolutions in modern political history, the French Revolution in the period 1789–1799 was the first attempt at popular democracy. France was under the influence of the Age of Enlightenment thinkers, and revolutionary zeal was the order of the day. Many of the *philosophes*, as the thinkers of that era are called, believed, however, in authority and did not support the idea of a takeover by the masses. But the political consciousness and opening up that they brought in, combined with a fiscal crisis and inflation that France faced at the time, made it easy to spark a revolution. This led to a violent overthrow of the monarchy, starting with the establishment of an Assembly in 1789. A constitution was drafted proclaiming equality of all citizens, establishing basic human rights, and putting an end to feudalism and the hegemony of the Church and nobility. However, what followed was no different from what has been happening in poor African or Asian nations upon introduction of popular democracy amidst poverty.

While at the start of the revolution nearly half the adult males could vote, by 1792, this right had been extended to all males. However, the Assembly lacked a unified voice and was dominated by a conflict between the conservatives and the radicals. This period was mired in anarchy, fractious infighting and violence. In 1793 the radical Jacobins assumed power and unleashed a "reign of terror"[1] with large scale arrests and executions as a means of "saving the revolution." This was followed by several weak governments. France also waged successful but costly wars on neighbors while domestic chaos and economic decline continued.

As in many poor democracies today, and maybe even in the prosperous ones, rumor and ignorance played a significant part in popular politics. Even in the storming of the fortress of Bastille, popularly seen as a symbol of despotism, in reality only seven inmates were allegedly found.[2] Likewise, in the rural areas, poor vagrants scouring for food and work were mistaken for armed agents of landlords hired to destroy crops and harass the common people. And thus the peasants, gripped by a panic, "the Great Fear," attacked the residences of their landlords. Danton, a justice minister of the new regime and allegedly in the pay of London, now instigated fear among the masses that counter-revolutionaries were planning to undermine the whole revolution. Easily aroused, the crowds stormed Parisian jails, mutilating and murdering over a thousand prisoners who were no mutineers but were just serving time for petty crimes.

Such forms of mob fury based on rumors are common occurrences in poor democracies of our times, too.

The revolutionary government was also a machinery of war. While Austria and Prussia had shown little interest to intervene in France's affairs, radical politicians like Brissot exaggerated the Austrian threat to the revolution and used this fear psychosis to generate support for declaring war on Austria. Many French-style revolutionary wars followed all over Europe. Ultimately, democracy sabotaged itself and growing anarchy, violence and poverty led to a coup that brought Napoleon Bonaparte to power in 1799, leading to a military dictatorship with powers more absolute than even most kings had enjoyed before.

While much poetic significance has been attached to the Revolution, in effect it bred the same chaotic factionalism, violence, mob rule and loss of human rights that we see in the myriad poor nations that turn to popular democracy today. France deserves a lot of credit for modern civilization concepts as its pioneering thinkers contributed to new political ideas in the Age of Reason, but the violent revolution that followed, not by design

1 "The French Revolution: The Radical Stage, 1792–1794," Steven Kreis, *The History Guide*, http://www.historyguide.org/intellect/lecture13a.html
2 The French Revolution, Thomas E. Kaizer, Microsoft® Encarta® Online Encyclopedia 2009

though, ended that age. A much more pragmatic and long lasting form to democracy was given shape by countries like the US and the UK, which gradually extended voting rights in line with economic development. That led to stable and progressive governments, and the path to universal suffrage took more than a century to unfold. In essence, France was a pioneer of thought but in reality a victim of its circumstances. The resultant outcome was not too unlike what happens in most poor nations of our times when they adopt popular democracy.

Spain is another country that chose a direct shortcut to universal suffrage over slow and steady evolution This was tried with disastrous results in 1873 and then again in 1931, the second time leading to a civil war and the ascent of Francisco Franco. However, during the latter half of Franco's rule, Spain industrialized rapidly and the democracy ushered in this time, after his demise in 1975, has been relatively stable.

Political empowerment becomes meaningful only if it follows economic empowerment. By itself, the right to vote is not empowerment; in fact if given prematurely, can lead to its subversive abuse. There are factors other than presence of a middle class and economic empowerment that enable a progressive democracy. A society must undergo certain social processes for democracy to work. In the West the Scientific Revolution, the Renaissance and the Age of Enlightenment emphasized the role of science and reason over dogmas, as well as respect for human rights and dignity. The role of religion in politics was also severely curtailed. However even if a society has undergone the social and intellectual revolution, if the poor still form the majority, democracy does not work—as was the case in post-revolutionary France.

Further, the transition from a centralized state authority to decentralized power in the hands of the people was a long journey in the West, stretching over centuries. The end result looked attractive and the developing nations adopted this political model as it is, upon attaining independence in the last century. But since democracy is rule by the majority, in whatever shape or form they may be, the character of these democracies was markedly different from that of the developed world. As explored here and will be further examined, there are many factors why democracy did not stabilize in the developing world and indeed destabilized many of the peaceful nations. Prima facie, the evidence thus far points towards universal suffrage democracy playing a detrimental role in the developing world. But let us examine this hypothesis further and try to unravel the reasons for it. Once we abandon our intuitive theories, and accept facts for what they are, we are making the right beginning—the right solutions will emerge.

CHAPTER 2. DEMOCRACY DERAILS DEVELOPMENT: HOW AND WHY?

Till about two centuries back, most societies were sharply polarized with a tiny wealthy class at the top and a large poor multitude at the bottom. Even the developed nations of today were like that, with the rural poor accounting for about 70% of the population. However, the 19th century changed the path of these nations, transforming them into prosperous societies with a middle class as its predominant core. What exactly did they do right and what factors helped these nations reach their developed status? Why is the developing world lagging far behind—is it just a matter of time or are they on the wrong path altogether? What role has democracy played in the development economics? With all its impending problems, is industrialization the only way forward; why can't we stay agrarian and develop? There is a lot of debate on inequality in the developed nations—are they really a good role model to follow? The answers to these questions will help clarify the political and economic way forward for the developing world.

THE COURSE OF DEMOCRACY AND DEVELOPMENT IN THE WEST

Whether or not democracy is the right model to follow, there is a need for a clearer understanding of the political economic dynamic that prevailed in the developed nations *while they were developing*. There may be insights we have failed to grasp which could be instrumental in addressing development issues of poor nations in the present context.

Britain started industrializing in the late 18ᵗʰ century. The farms got bigger in size, and productivity increased, leading to huge gains in food production—and a reduced need for farm labor. The rural poor, hitherto living on subsistence farming, started migrating to the cities in search of jobs. Between 1801 and 1851, the population of towns such as Liverpool and Manchester grew by 1,000 percent. Town authorities found it impossible to regulate the population explosion[1]. Landlords constructed ramshackle housing simply to provide shelter. Thousands lived in basements without light or heat, with appalling sanitary conditions, and disease outbreaks were common. This bears a striking resemblance to the urban slums that are all too familiar with in the developing world of today.

Initially, most of the gains accrued mainly to the factory owning classes. But despite theories of gloom and doom and a belief that the rich will get richer and the poor poorer, general living standards started rising across classes towards the latter half of the 19ᵗʰ century. As the system started to stabilize, working conditions improved, child labor was banned and education and enterprise became the means to growth. Living conditions as well as the general health and well being of the populace went up considerably. Contrary to what was earlier passionately believed and propagated, everybody got richer—some much more than the others, but the poor did not get poorer. Even today inequality is lower in industrialized developed countries than in rest of the world. For instance in 1999 dollar terms, in the 31 developed nations of the OECD, about 40% of the national income is earned by the top quintile whereas the same figure for the whole world is about 70%. Likewise the Gini inequality coefficient is lower for North America and Europe than for other continents or regions.[2]

Noteworthy is the fact that as Britain and other nations went through their development pangs, they did not have democracy. Voting rights were limited to wealthy males and extended gradually over a century, in line with economic empowerment. All the societal tensions and conflicts that exist in poor nations when they start the process of industrialization existed in Britain too, in the early stages. But since voting rights were limited, devel-

---

1 History of the United Kingdom, Mark Kishlansky, Microsoft® Encarta® Online Encyclopedia 2009

2 Poverty Around the World, Anup Shah, Global Issues, 2010, http://www.globalissues.org/article/4/poverty-around-the-world

opment proceeded at a fast pace and was not derailed. Industrialization led to the emergence or considerable expansion of a new middle class that earned its living in trade or professions like law, teaching and medicine; this was also a class that valued literacy, thrift and education.

Only in the 20th century was democracy as we know it today, with universal voting rights, ushered in. Power came to rest in the hands of the middle class which had already formed a majority in the society. Market economy thus has been the first leveler, transforming societies polarized between extremely rich and poor to graded societies with three different classes predominant one being the Middle. No doubt the developed nations too have issues of their own but if any of the developing nations can reach that status on economic or human development parameters, the world would be a nicer place. Free markets based industrialization is certainly a proven way forward but why is it in conflict with democracy? What are the alternatives anyway?

WHY INDUSTRIALIZE, WHY NOT STAY AGRARIAN AND DEVELOP?

Harmony with nature, which has been greatly disturbed by industrialization and consumerism, ought to remain an important goal to strive for. But does that mean nations that are largely rural should stay that way and industrialization is an evil to be avoided? Also, since a large percentage of the developing world population is engaged in agriculture does that not mean we have to focus on agriculture not industries, as is often propounded by opinion leaders in these nations? Why does development have to mean industrialization; can we not stay agrarian and develop? Is it possible to eradicate poverty through focus on agriculture itself? What, if anything, is wrong with that logic?

It is important first to understand who the agricultural economies of the world are and what kind of net contribution the sector makes to their overall economy and employment generation. In terms of agricultural output, the US and the European Union together account for nearly 22% of the world's produce. But agriculture contributes to less than 2% of their

GDP[1] and employs only about 1–8% of the population.[2] Agriculture in these nations is centered round large farms that use machinery as well as technical and marketing know-how. The other end of the spectrum are poor countries like Afghanistan, Burundi, Angola, Zambia, etc., where 80% of the population is engaged in agriculture, but the sector's contribution to their own meager GDPs is between 20 and 40% and to the world total agro-produce, almost negligible. Many of these poor nations consider themselves agrarian economies but in fact they are merely agrarian, not economies. The biggest agricultural producers still are the US, the EU and the emergent nations like China, India and Brazil. Of the latter, China has become one of the largest agricultural producers as well as donors[3] in the world. As happened in the developed nations, in China too the increase in farm output has gone up in tandem with a huge decline in the proportion of population engaged in agriculture, dropping from over 70% in 1978 to just 23% of the population or about 36% of the labor force in 2009. Yet, agriculture contributes only 12% to its GDP. At the aggregate level too, agriculture contributes a meager 4% to the world GDP. A century or so prior, agriculture was a predominant sector and agrarian economies like Argentina were among the most prosperous in the world. But they were left far behind by nations in Europe, North America and the Pacific which expanded and widened their industrial base. Today value added goods and services contribute the most to the world GDP. Commodities-based agriculture remains a small proportion of world economy, a mere 4%, and thus cannot provide remunerative employment to large bases of population. Food is a basic necessity and agriculture should always be a focus sector but in today's context, it can never be the mainstay of an economy.

The message here is for all poor nations with large bases of population engaged in agriculture where there are many misconceptions that maybe these governments have to focus on agriculture as the prime growth sector. That is a myth. The fate of agriculture is large farms that can use machines, technological and marketing know-how. In the West, industrialization

---

1 Nominal GDP Sector composition for countries, 2005, Compiled from CIA World Factbook, http://en.wikipedia.org/wiki/List_of_countries_by_GDP_sector_composition

2 Employment in Agriculture, World Development Indicators, 2008, The World Bank, http://data.worldbank.org/indicator/SL.AGR.EMPL.ZS

3 China emerges as world's third largest food aid donor, World Food program, 20 Jul 2006, http://www.wfp.org/node/534

precipitated a large scale migration to cities in search of jobs as the farms got bigger and more mechanized. They started using scientific methods in demand prediction, made more efficient use of water and soil, and employed pest control products. As a result food production soared, eliminating the large scale famine threats that had haunted mankind since times immemorial. In the poor nations, the farms are small, farmers often debt ridden, relying on primitive wasteful methods and dependent on the vagaries of nature, making farming a risky but non remunerative[1] business. If poverty has to be reduced, it means the agricultural community has to be moved to other avenues and that can be accelerated by the spread of industries as well as educational opportunities. Short term relief may be provided but the long term fate of the agricultural community is to move to other sectors.

The charm that an urbane intellectual finds in an un-spoilt rural existence is largely based on ignorance. Living in rural poverty means not having access to safe water or nutrition, electricity, sanitation facilities, medical care or education, losing children to diseases, and escaping into alcoholism and violence. It is just primal existence—charming only to the outsider, not the one who has to live it. Development and industrialization go together. Environmental consciousness remains an important goal, but leaving people poor, destitute and backward isn't the answer to concerns over environment protection.

WHAT ROLE DOES DEMOCRACY PLAY IN THE DEVELOPMENT PROCESS?

As happened in the West, wealth creation in a market economy follows an exponential curve—initially the gains are small and a handful benefit but once it gains momentum, prosperity grows wider and wider. The exact opposite is true of a centrally controlled command economy—there are immediate benefits for the needy but as it progresses, everything declines, and sharply too. But development works like a ripple effect, reaching different strata of the society in different stages and the early gainers are bitterly resented. This happened in the Western nations too in the early stages of industrialization. But development per se was not halted as these nations did not have full democracy when they went through that phase; voting rights

---

1 Small farmers get bulk of their income from non-agriculture activities, Sandip Das, The Financial Express, 2009, http://www.financialexpress.com/news/small-farmers-get-bulk-of-their-income-from-nonagriculture-activities/519810/

were limited. Most developing nations get stuck in the initial phase itself with massive resistance to industrialization as well as infrastructure creation. Both are summarily dismissed as pro-rich. Let us look at an example from India to understand the why and how of it.

About 72% of India is rural and almost 40% of farmers have expressed an interest to be out of farming[1]. The economic opportunities continue to be concentrated around the metros that seem to be bursting at seams. To spread industrialization further and farther, the government tried to set up Special Economic Zones (SEZs) in remote parts of the country. This led to an almost violent opposition. The reason touted was that agricultural land was being diverted to industries and corporations were taking away the rights of the farmers. These are mainly emotional arguments, as industry is not an intensive land use exercise. All of the 540 odd proposed SEZs will take away only a small fraction, about 0.06%, of arable land or about 0.03% of the total land in India.[2] Rajiv Kumar, Director of Indian Council for Research on International Economic Relations (ICRIER), questions then, where is the trade off? Yet, as he says, this kind of unsubstantiated and almost irrelevant debate has become quite common in our country[3]. But emotionally-charged arguments continue unabated and win favor with the populace. Many plants have been shut down and almost all new projects stalled thus. However the same farmers go back to a desperate existence with escalating suicides at the rate of about 20,000 per annum[4], and the government gets blamed for doing nothing about that. So what was the point in opposing industrialization? Why is the vehicle of employment generation misconstrued as one of exploitation?

Urbanization continues to be thwarted[5] and here again, a comparison with China is inevitable. In 1951, merely 17% of India's population was urban

1 "Agriculture — Grain Drain, Raj Chengappa with Ramesh Vinayak", *India Today*, 11 Jun 2007, http://www.india-today.com/itoday/20070611/cover1.html

2 "Experts see Gujarat as SEZ capital of India, Gaurav Sharma," *Indian Express*, 12 Mar 2009, http://www.indianexpress.com/news/experts-see-gujarat-as-sez-capital-of-india/409641/

3 "Can the SEZ policy undermine agriculture?" Rajiv Kumar, *The Economic Times*, 3 Oct 2006, http://economictimes.indiatimes.com/articleshow/msid-2069754,curpg-3.cms

4 "Agriculture — Grain Drain," Raj Chengappa with Ramesh Vinayak, *India Today*, 2007, http://www.india-today.com/itoday/20070611/cover1.html

5 India Needs Cities Network for Easy Rural — Urban Shift, Economy and Politics, livemint.com, http://www.livemint.com/2009/08/03224002/India-needs-cities-network-for.html

and the corresponding figure for China was even lower at 13%. In the developing world, rural usually means lack of water supply, electricity, drainage, schools, roads, law and order, medical facilities, etc. It is less like living amidst nature and more like primate existence. The rate of urbanization remained low in both the nations and by 1991 they were equal at about 26%. However China took a big leap after that as its urban population[1] jumped to 36% by 2001 and then further to 47% by 2009, whereas India stayed more or less where it was with only about 28% urban even today. Of this just the top 10 cities account for 70% of India's GDP[2] while large tracts of rural India remain devoid of any employment opportunities. The urban leap for China came from expanded industrial opportunities as its poor rural low-skilled class found gainful employment in factories. As a result, the industrial sector contributes about 48% of its GDP. The corresponding figure for India remained 19%. India too has a large base of poor rural low-skilled people but in the absence of industrialization, they have no credible employment avenues. However, the people as well as their opinion leaders stand firmly in the path of development, demanding time and again to somehow magically turn agriculture into the most remunerative industry in the world; which is not possible.

In one of the Indian states of Gujarat, SEZ-based industrialization has been adopted with enthusiasm. It led to creation of 1 million jobs in a span of just two years. Of the jobs thus created, 70% were in the manufacturing sector, most likely to benefit the rural uneducated poor. It is estimated that every 25 acres in a manufacturing SEZ generates 5000 jobs[3], on a conservative basis, as compared to 5 farm workers[4] that would have been employed on a farm of that size.

This kind of a societal conflict over industrialization happened in the Western nations too, in the early part of the 19th century, but they did not have to convince the entire rural poor populace of the long term benefits of it. The poor, now as then, view development with suspicion, believing

1 Urban and Rural Population in China 1978 and 2002, Tables, Figures and Maps, China Profile, http://www.china-profile.com/data/tab_rurpop_1.htm

2 GDP—The Top 10 Cities in India, 23 Apr 2010, rediff.com, http://business.rediff.com/slide-show/2010/apr/23/slide-show-1-the-top-10-cities-in-india-by-gdp.htm

3 "Looking for a job, Gujarat awaits you," *The Economic Times*, 31 Aug 2006, http://economictimes.indiatimes.com/news/economy/indicators/Looking-for-a-job-Gujarat-awaits-you/articleshow/1941591.cms

4 Number of workers per farm, *Rural Sociology in India* (p. 310), A R Desai, The Indian Society of Agricultural Economy

it will never benefit them. This insecurity is further fuelled by opposition parties, activists and even portions of media who after all has been said and shown, do believe in their hearts the rich will get richer and the poor poorer. In reality it is lack of industrialization that would make the poor poorer. Some of the non democratic nations like China are fast industrializing and maximizing benefits from global low cost manufacturing opportunities. But the democratic developing nations are caught in a vicious cycle of opposition and deliberations.

While development is opposed, the need for instant gratification dominates the voters demands. There is a tendency to demand everything "free" from the government. And increasingly the governments that oblige with freebies like bags of rice, saris, cash, loan waivers, etc., are termed "pro-people". In reality these are just short term programs that instill scope for corruption as political middle men hack away at the sums being doled out. When the government follows a more long term and prudent approach of working through the economy or investing in infrastructure, it gets labeled as "pro-rich". Democracy, as of now, stands firmly in the path of development, daring it to turn back, unaware and ignorant that it is the only savior that will rescue it from destitution and poverty.

DEMOCRACY AND POVERTY ALLEVIATION—THE ALTERNATIVES

There is no doubt that the first objective before most developing nations is to reduce abject poverty—the huge tracts of population who are living below the poverty line. The mechanism to break out of poverty as used in the Western nations was large scale industrialization using a market economy model. But that need not be the only way; let us examine some of the alternative poverty alleviation programs that have been tried thus far.

The first alternative tried was a centrally controlled command economy like in Soviet Russia. In these economies, the state decided what should be produced, how much, and where. This was not based on demand but on social objectives, like which regions to boost by increasing employment opportunities. This resulted in production facilities being built far away from the markets for the goods produced, adding huge transportation costs. Production quotas as well as reporting of actual production became corrupt with manipulation of figures and money changing hands. And then, psychologically, the system was an assurance to everyone that they were all equal and that the state assumed responsibility for them. When major projects like railroads had to be built, people resisted, having quickly adopted the notion that the State would "provide." Ultimately a lot of forced cheap labor was used to do the construction. The same or similar was also true of China, Cuba, etc. For instance, Castro and Guevara attempted to use the New Man Theory to motivate Cubans to work harder for the revolution. It did not prove successful. Although working-class and poor Cubans supported the goals of the revolution, many were not willing to work long hours without increased financial compensation[1]. The system resulted in overall poor efficiency and a huge bureaucratic machinery which became corrupt. Finally the economy collapsed and led to everyone becoming poor (other than the ruling party bosses and other such *éminences grises*). So it achieved greater poverty, tyranny and continued inequality where the nobility of yesteryears just got replaced by despotic party bosses. Poverty reduction could not be achieved through these command control economies.

Let us look at a recent example from India of a huge poverty alleviation initiative launched by the Indian government in 2005, the National Rural Employment Guarantee Act (NREGA). In response to the lack of employment opportunities in the largely poor and destitute rural India and at the urging of activists who opposed SEZs, the government passed the NREGA which guarantees a minimum 100 days employment to all rural households at the minimum wage rate. The work is left to local bodies to decide and output expectations are not clear. The central government outlay for the scheme is $8 billion for the full year 2009-2010 and it is estimated that this project may cost up to 5% of the GDP. Now coming to the implementation, which is the main problem in all such schemes. Corruption and discrimination has already seeped into the project. Making a job card requires bribes ranging from Rs5-50 and caste, gender and religion based discrimination has been noticed. The benefits have been cornered by local powerful elements and better off sections in the villages leaving the lowest castes, women (particularly widows) as well as the below poverty line populace relatively untouched[2]. Social audits reveal that the number of job cards issued have been in excess of numbers employed, indicating that the funds have been embezzled by local officials. Now the blame game has started

1 History of Cuba, Microsoft® Encarta® Online Encyclopedia 2009

2 The Indian NREGA: Will it reduce poverty and boost the economy? Disa Sjoblom and John Farrington, Overseas Development Institute, UK, 2008, http://www.odi. org.uk/resources/download/440.pdf

putting onus on the bureaucracy or corruption. But was it not expected? As concluded by Disa Sjoblom and John Farrington of Overseas Development Institute, "Except for isolated instances, there is little evidence that NREGA is being implemented better than the panoply of poverty-focused schemes introduced by the government of India over the past 20 years, where a large share of intended benefits have been captured by the elite classes, including petty functionaries." Despite limited resources and huge dependence on oil imports, the government could be commended for at least trying to run poverty alleviation programs but they seem like wasteful and inefficient use of meager resources. This costly initiative is also at a time when India is facing large budget deficits[1] as well as a ballooning debt problem. Ultimately, this kind of reckless spending without any long term payoffs leads to an inflationary economy as has already happened.

Likewise in Venezuela, a massive pro poor program was launched by Hugo Chavez with government sponsored free distribution of food and money for the needy. Further, large farms are being broken up, with fragments distributed to landless farmers. But ownership of agricultural property as a key to empowerment is an obsolete concept. Over two centuries back, agriculture was the main source of employment or remuneration. Today, rather than being sent back to farms, the farmers ought to be moved to other avenues of employment which can come about by spreading industries. While all this has helped catapult Hugo Chavez to a hero-like status, Venezuela is facing acute food shortages as well as an inflation rate higher than the rest of Latin America.

There are two key issues why such government sponsored free distribution of benefits and cash has not worked in alleviating poverty in the developing world. One, the delivery mechanism itself is faulty. When poverty and corruption is widespread and law enforcement weak, the welfare benefits given by state or even charitable organizations tend to get usurped by middle men and lead to corrupt inefficient use of the already stretched and meager resources. Two, these are struggling small economies with large population bases. So, wealth has to be created first before being distributed. Not having yet developed an economic base, they ultimately start printing money to fund their pro poor programs, leading to inflation, as has already

---

1 Budget deficits and national debt, Martin Feldstein, Reserve Bank of India, 2004, http://rbi.org.in/Scripts/PublicationsView.aspx?Id=5915. India's deficit can't be sustained at this level, 2010, Gulfnews, http://gulfnews.com/business/economy/india-s-deficit-can-t-be-sustained-at-this-level-1.560857

happened in Venezuela. To create wealth through an egalitarian model, many of the developing countries nationalized industries in the 1960s and 1970s. This uniformly led to sluggish economies, greater bureaucracy, inflation and in the case of Latin America, hyperinflation. Wealth creation was made possible only post their market oriented economic reforms and liberalization. On the other hand, many of the Western developed nations especially in Europe have successfully evolved mixed economy models and instituted extensive welfare benefits, but mainly in their post industrial phase. When their economic base was weak and pockets largely empty, they did not develop using such models.

However this is not to say this can not be improved upon and we see how China has done it; but before that let us examine in simple plain terms how a decentralized economy alleviates poverty. Let us say a few factories are opened in a rural area. Apart from direct employment as industrial labor, a lot of secondary and tertiary employment is generated. People come to live there and houses etc. have to be built, someone opens tea stalls, small eateries, someone caters to the factory canteens, housekeeping jobs are created, and small shops will open. Employment is created, in a sustainable manner; no supervision is required, people get paid for the work and initiative and it remains largely corruption free. Further, it would not put a burden on the already stretched exchequer; instead the government earns taxes from these business operations. Employment generation thus becomes the prime means of alleviating poverty.

In China, the government experimented with such a decentralized system in a few SEZs at first and then scaled it up to almost the whole of economy. Yet instead of relying purely on market forces, it directly invested heavily in infrastructure and education as opposed to free distribution of money or benefits to alleviate poverty. As per the World Bank, between 1981 and 2005, the world poverty rate fell by about 25%. China accounted for most of that as its population living in poverty fell from 85% to just 15.9%. Roughly 600 million people were delivered from abject poverty,[1] defined as $1.25 per day. We examine this model in greater detail later on.

So, in essence, creating genuine employment opportunities through a robust economy seems to be the means of alleviating large scale poverty.

---

1 "World Bank's Poverty Estimates Revised," Anup Shah, Aug 2008, *Global Issues*, http://www.globalissues.org/article/4/poverty-around-the-world#WorldBanksP overtyEstimatesRevised

Just giving people money or pots of soup occasionally, "while stocks last," does not pull them out of poverty. This mechanism of distributing money or benefits as a means to poverty alleviation in the developing world only benefits the political parties that espouse such programs. They win instant support and don the roles of people's messiahs. The common (poor) man too understands when something comes to him for free and, desperate in his meager existence, he also relates readily to the anti rich rhetoric. He does not understand how a market economy and its "invisible hand" is going to benefit him. Even in China the development and the resultant poverty alleviation program met with tremendous resistance and people did not support it initially, but the program was not derailed as Chinese leaders do not have to campaign for votes.

A market economy is not without its ills and has abundant scope for improvement and challenge. Debates about the nature and degree of markets regulation, government intervention and investments in long term programs, or altogether new models continue and ought to especially in the developed world. But even with all its imperfections, as a first step out of poverty, a decentralized market economy is still the best model and the only one that has worked thus far. While endeavors to make "free markets" more equitable and fair or experimentation with alternative models may continue in line with social objectives, that is an issue for the developed nations to resolve. There is a dichotomy between priorities before the developed versus the developing world. In the former, issues about inequality are crucial but in the developing world, the first problem and priority is removal of desperate abject large scale poverty and restoring basic dignity to this population. The society still is sharply polarized and a turn to a market economy would allow them to become a more graded society of three classes, with a majority centered in the middle. That is a dream for any developing nation and we should not confuse ourselves with issues troubling the developed world and reject the tried and tested model per se.

Industrialization does pose challenges that ought to be addressed but the solution is not to avoid development altogether, leaving people destitute and agrarian. All the developed nations have followed a decentralized market economy as their basic poverty alleviation model and overall that is what has been the defining point between developed and under developed countries, not democracy.

It might not be stretching the truth to say that market economy is a precursor to, as well as an enabler of, democracy. Unless wealth is created in a widespread manner and a society has a strong middle class, democracy of the poor is subversive and self destructive. But due to its very nature of unequal rewards, the "free market" economy often comes into conflict with democracy. So it remains an over-vilified system and its role as the first leveler in a polarized largely poor society has gone unrecognized. Instead of chasing mirages, the developing world would benefit greatly by focusing on the problems of extreme poverty and destitution and use this tried and tested formula to come up to a decent level of human existence. The priorities here are different from those of the developed world. A lot of governments in the developing countries understand this well but find it nearly impossible to educate the vast rural poor as to the long term economic implications of different systems. In such a case, alternate political mechanisms need to be evolved such that development programs are not derailed.

CHAPTER 3. OTHER SYSTEMS: LESSONS YET UNLEARNT

Democracy has many deficiencies—but in comparison to what, it should be asked. Before we examine democracy's pitfalls and shortcomings in depth, let us assess what alternate models have to offer first. That would set a backdrop for relative assessment of democracy as well as provide pointers for way forward in the developing world. Further, countries like Afghanistan and Pakistan have come to symbolize terrorism and violence, posing a threat to themselves as well as the world at large. Why are they like this, or more importantly, were they always like this? It may surprise or even shock a good majority of people to know that many of these nations were utterly peaceful, with a fair sprinkling of progressive leaders, not too long ago.

What changed them and brought them to the brink of a disaster? It is just a present biased prejudice that all these nations had tyrannies before and are now venturing on a progressive path with a quest for democracy. "Reality" is in stark contrast to this belief. Just as democracy is over-glorified with its weaknesses pushed under the carpet, other systems have been over-vilified with many of their strengths unrecognized and unacknowledged. Even so, the idea is not to use convoluted logic to go back to tyrannies but it is an assertion here that history has many lessons relevant to our times that have been ignored, misrepresented or simply left out in the cold to suit our present thinking. Let us hear them for once.

Other than democracy, the systems that have been around are Aristocracy, Military Rule, Single Party Rule and Oligarch Republics. Let us see what, if anything, we can distill from them to meet our present political needs. Going from the most centralized to the least:

ARISTOCRACY / MONARCHY

Their time is gone and hopefully will never come back again, but a fairer assessment in the contemporary context may help enhance our understanding of some of our present problems. Early 20th century, the Middle East was undergoing a transformation of sorts with reformist leaders trying to modernize and industrialize their nations, all while being fiercely secularist. Kemal Atatürk in Turkey was one example of that and Reza Shah Pahlavi[1] in Iran another. The lesser known case is that of Afghanistan.

Afghanistan

Afghanistan has been made notorious by terrorism and the Taliban but very few people perhaps know that the nation was under a stable monarchy for most of the last century. Let us try to solve the riddle of how it regressed into the present state by looking at its past.[2] Afghanistan began the last century on a great note with progressive rulers following in each other's stead, one after the other. Abdur Rahman Khan, known as Iron Amir, united the fragmented nation as Afghanistan. His son, who ruled from 1901 till 1919, took the first steps towards the introduction of modern education and industry. His son and successor Amanullah Khan,[3] who became Emir in 1919 and Shah or king in 1926, had even more ambitious plans for modernizing the state. He undertook a literacy drive, introduced reforms and encouraged women to give up the veil. This offended the religious leaders and revolts broke out, forcing Amanullah to flee the country in 1929. Zahir Shah came to power in 1933 and ruled for 40 years. He was a moderate reformer and Afghanistan enjoyed peace and quiet under him. In the 1960s he made some reforms to establish a primal form of constitutional monarchy and granted suffrage to women as well. In 1973, his cousin, Mohammed Daoud, overthrew the Shah. But even Daoud favored modernization and women's emancipation.

---

1   Reza Shah, Wikipedia, the free encyclopedia, http://en.wikipedia.org/wiki/Reza_Shah_Pahlavi
2   History of Afghanistan, Microsoft® Encarta® Online Encyclopedia 2009
3   Amanullah Khan, Wikipedia, the free encyclopedia, http://en.wikipedia.org/wiki/Amanullah_Khan

In 1978, the communists took up the reins but soon got caught in factional infighting. In character with communist ideology, however, they supported equality, including women's rights, and opposed religious influence on the society.

Post 1979, however, Afghanistan's development and stability were destroyed as Russia invaded it and the US supported a *mujahideen* insurgency from Pakistan. From this point onwards, the nation was played as a pawn in the cold war between the US and the USSR. The Taliban was a later offshoot of the *mujahideen* insurgents that took control of Afghanistan in the 1990s. Post 2001, the nation was invaded by US and allied forces, after the September 11 disasters. In 2004, it was turned into a democracy amidst ongoing war. The nation has continued its steep decline into terrorism, violence, poverty and anarchy. It is important to reflect on this evidence that most Afghani leaders from the royal family, as well as the communists, believed in modern education and championed women's rights in an otherwise deeply conservative society. Most importantly, the monarchy especially kept the nation stable and progressive. Today the nation has turned into a rudimentary quasi democracy in the hands of local uneducated regressive tribal warlords who are dragging the nation backwards.

Aristocracy essentially is an archaic, redundant form, where the royalty assumes an elevated social status. There is one set of laws for the populace and another or none for them. It could easily be an arbitrary rule by decrees and thus needed changing. But with the benefit of hindsight, nations with stable monarchiess should have adopted an evolutionary approach similar to that of the UK. Evolving from absolute monarchy to constitutional monarchy to limited suffrage parliamentary democracy, stretching over perhaps a century or so, would likely have kept them stable and relatively more progressive.

MILITARY RULE

Most democracies in the developing world regularly alternate with military rules, the latter often providing greater stability and progress than the former. Military rule has many weaknesses and thus can never be the recommended long term system, but there are a lot of misunderstandings about it which need to be cleared. Military takeover is not about hunger for power; usually the military heads have enough power as they have had successful careers and enjoyed enough privileges. By the very nature of their jobs, most are also patriotic. Their motive usually is a need to restore order amidst chaos. This social and political chaos, crime and corruption could be a result of anything, but in the last century it often has been a byproduct of mass democracy. Military is about discipline and control and usually, the rulers takeover with a view to establishing the same order in the civil society at large. At times the public even applauds such a rescue operation. Military rulers are often broadminded, support women's rights and discourage religious manipulation of power. Their biggest flaw however is that they also tend to be autocratic. Nations like Pakistan, that are core to the war on terror, have had military rulers and understanding the political dynamic there may help find solution to problems that plague such nations and in turn, the entire world.

Pakistan

Unlike India, where the Nehru–Gandhi led Congress party stabilized the diverse Indian democracy, keeping the nation together post independence, Pakistan's founder Muhammad Ali Jinnah, who could have been its potential anchor, died a year after independence. Since then, the nation has oscillated between military rule and democratic regimes. While most of its democratic leaders have been mired in corruption scandals and divisive politics, Pakistan's more enlightened rulers have come from the military. Right in the beginning, Ayub Khan rescued the nation from chaos and political infighting in 1958, and he stabilized the fledgling nation. The following decade when military was in power, Pakistan knew relative peace and progress. A more recent example deserving better scrutiny is that of its last military ruler, Pervez Musharraf. He ascended to power in 1999 post a democratic decade that was fraught with fractious infighting and weak leadership. At the time, Pakistan was in deep economic turmoil and was one of the most highly indebted nations in the world. During his nine years' rule, Musharraf put Pakistan back on track. The economy doubled in size and so did per capita income and exports. Foreign reserves grew five times and there was improvement across all economic parameters.[1]

---

1 Pakistan Economy, Economic indicators, 2001–2010, Board of Investment, Government of Pakistan, http://www.pakboi.gov.pk/eco-ind.htm, Achievements of Pervez Musharraf's government, Industry & Economy, Pakistan's business magazine, http://www.pakistaneconomist.com/issue2000/issue45/i&e3.htm

Musharraf joined hands with the US in the war on terror, despite objections within his country. One of the greatest acts he did was to promote human rights for women by amending the *Hudood* ordinance. It was a draconian law that required a woman to produce four chaste Muslim men as eye witnesses to prove a rape case, failing which she was imprisoned for adultery. A vast majority of women in jails were serving time on this account. Fearful of the clerics, the prior democratic regimes including that of the "woman" PM, Benazir Bhutto, had only paid lip service to women's rights but done nothing to change it. Musharraf stood up to the clerics and fundamentalist elements in the society and introduced a women's protection bill[1] to counter the *Hudood* law. He also made advances in literacy improvement as well as setting up 47 new universities. He was a progressive ruler who had put Pakistan's economy as well as security back on track. However a battle with the chief justice of Pakistan Supreme Court finally proved too costly for him and he had to make way for democracy under internal and external pressure.

Having reverted to democracy, Pakistan has slipped back into lawlessness and terror groups are thriving under that kind of a decentralized weak system. This is nothing new to Pakistan; almost all of its past democratic eras have bred chaos and violence. It begs mention here that not all previous military regimes have been as enlightened. Zia ul Haq, who staged a coup in 1977 and stayed in power till his death, was a despotic ruler and also was the one who brought in several barbaric laws like the Hudood. But the democratic regimes that followed took the nation to a much lower level and were the ones to support insurgency in Kashmir as well as Afghanistan. Even today upon return to democracy, Pakistan is fast descending into chaos and violence as insurgency has gained ground.

Pervez Musharraf is not a one-off instance; a great majority of rulers from the military have tended towards modernization, scientific education, secularism and women's rights. The most respectable amongst these was Kemal Atatürk, considered the founder of modern Turkey. He broadedned the base of education, encouraged women's emancipation and worked towards Turkey's integration with the global world. In Bangladesh too, the last military rulers tried to bring order[2] and weed out corruption and de-

---

1 Musharraf signs women's protection bill, *Dawn*, 2006, http://www.dawn.com/2006/12/02/top7.htm

2 Bangladesh: Caretaker Government Targets Dynastic Politics, Anand Kumar, 18 Apr 2007, South Asia Analysis Group, http://www.southasiaanalysis.

manded some basic educational standards from the religious schools called *Madrasas*. In contrast, the democracy there has been dynastic in nature, corrupt and ineffective in dealing with poverty or religious violence.

Military rulers tend to focus on law and order, secularism, women's rights, as well as education, as we shall see in many examples later on too.

Myanmar

And now for a controversial example. Myanmar (formerly known as Burma) has had a military rule since 1962. The democratic decade prior to that was chaotic, fraught with secessionist movements, drug trafficking and the last premier's attempt at making Buddhism the state religion. Heavy international sanctions have been imposed on Myanmar and its economy remains in shambles. While the regime is known for its crackdown on protesting monks, its achievements are pushed under the carpet. Since colonial times, Thailand, Laos and Myanmar together had been dubbed the golden triangle of opium cultivation. In 1999/2000 the military regime began implementation of a plan to eliminate drugs production in 15 years and sought $150 million assistance for alternate development of the region. They got 10% of that amount[1] and a load of sanctions, on account of "not being a democracy." NGOs from China and Japan, however, provided some developmental assistance to the country. As part of this drive, the regime cracked down on the drug mafias and handled the violent tendencies of such cartels effectively. The UN recognizes that the once notorious golden triangle has made a concerted effort to slash opium cultivation[2] to the extent that it now produces only 5% of the world's deadliest drug—the rest comes from Afghanistan.[3] Likewise the insurgency was controlled within and Myanmar also helped India rout insurgents in its bordering states. The secularist military regime has opposed theocratic tendencies in the state, which in fact was a trigger for the takeover. Since then, it has been resented by the religious establishment of monks with whom the military regime shares an uneasy relationship.

---

org/%5Cpapers23%5Cpaper2214.html

1 External help for drug fight at a low, Myanmar Government, 2000, http://www.myanmar.gov.mm/myanmartimes/no52/external_help.htm

2 Where has all the opium gone? Ron Gluckman, *Wall Street Journal*, 1995, http://www.gluckman.com/BurmaBorder.html

3 Afghanistan leads world in opium production — UN Report, 2007, CBC News, http://www.cbc.ca/world/story/2007/06/26/drug-report.html

What is the recommended alternative for Myanmar? Multiparty democracy with Aung San Suu Kyi as the leader is predictably the answer. Does anyone see similarities between this situation and Pakistan in 1988: hopeful revolutionary fervor for democracy and return of the slain leader's daughter, foreign educated, suave, a Western favorite at the time: Benazir Bhutto. Where did it take Pakistan? Aung San Suu Kyi shares a similar dynastic past, characteristic of most developing world democratic leaders. Her slain father was the founder of modern Myanmar. She is Oxford educated and till her return to elections had spent most of her life outside Myanmar. Her background gives her wide acceptability with the Western media and governments because she is someone they can easily relate to. She is no doubt a good philosopher and has to be commended for her peaceful protest as well as tremendous personal sacrifices. But it can be seriously doubted whether she would be able to control the fractious separatism and the drug trade that potentially exists in all the bordering regions of Myanmar and which would raise its ugly head in full force if the nation returns to multiparty democracy, like it did before.[1]

Myanmar is not a North Korea that has remained closed and refused to acknowledge the changing world outside or developed nuclear weapons. Myanmar faces sanctions just for not being a democracy. Upon bringing democracy, what is to stop it from becoming another Pakistan?

This argument is not intended to promote military rule but to highlight some aspects, very important ones at that, which biased international pressure groups fail to acknowledge, leave alone entertain. In the quest for truth, there are going to be such inconvenient revelations. The way forward for most of these nations is not a violent or revolutionary overthrow of the present centralized power structure but an evolutionary transition to progressively more open and decentralized systems.

SINGLE PARTY RULE

While the immediate example that comes to mind is China, single party rule indeed has been tried in quite a few other countries with great amount of success but has not received any recognition thus far. Let us look at a few of these examples.

---

1 What to do about Burma, Thant Myint-U, 2007, http://www.lrb.co.uk/v29/n03/-thantmyint-u/what-to-do-about-burma

Colombia

The mention of Colombia conjures up images of drugs cartels, FARC kidnappings, torture, and killings. However, even worse than this violence was the decade long bloodshed that started in 1948, a period known in Colombia as *La Violencia.*[1] The two parties, liberals and conservatives, with their respective supporters, engaged in a civil war claiming 180,000 lives. In 1957, leaders of the two political parties rescued the nation and arrived at an agreement to share all government offices equally and alternate the presidency between them. This arrangement of a unity government, called the National Front,[2] was also supported by a plebiscite. It came into effect in 1958 and lasted a good 16 years. This quickly brought an end to large scale violence that had become the mainstay of most Colombians' lives.

The ensuing period was one of unprecedented stability and progress as the government undertook social and economic reforms. In the 1960s, leftist guerrillas like FARC, inspired by the Cuban revolution, tried to destabilize the nation but were rendered ineffective by the strong unity rule. The government increased spending on education, health and housing but remained capitalist in essence and thus also received much assistance from the US. Unlike the rest of the continent, Colombia avoided the severe hyper inflation, upwards of even 1000%, suffered by most other Latin American countries at that time.

The effectiveness of this unity government becomes even more apparent when contrasted with what followed. In 1974 Colombia returned to democracy, elections and the associated fluid governance. This ushered in a new era of violence. Leftist guerrillas like the FARC and to a lesser extent ELN became powerful and in negotiations with weak changing governments, managed to carve out regions that became their fiefdoms. In response, scattered paramilitary groups formed all over the country intending to protect rural communities from guerrilla violence but soon themselves turned violent too. Since the 1980s Colombia also became a large exporter of illegal drugs, mainly cocaine. Along with that came the expected criminal estab-

---

[1] Colombia History, Charles Bergquist, Microsoft® Encarta® Online Encyclopedia 2009

[2] Colombia — National Front and economic Development, Bruce Michael Bagley, p124–142, Politics, policies and economic development in Latin America, Robert G Wesson, Hoover Press, 1984

lishments. Bombings, assassinations, kidnappings, and torture killings became commonplace.

Only after 2002 things started to improve with the rise of a strong president, Álvaro Uribe. He undertook a military operation against the rebels and brought them to the negotiation table. But his two-term limit bars him from contesting elections post 2010. A strong leader, Uribe has put Colombia's steep descent to lawlessness into reverse gear but it remains to be seen whether the peace and progress continues post 2010 under the fluid governance characteristic of typical democracies.

Spain

Spain had a tumultuous 19th century with repeated conflicts between the conservative and liberal factions. In 1873, Spain attempted its first universal male suffrage democracy, which only seemed to add to the prevailing conflict and chaos. This first Republic was full of disagreements and instability with four presidents coming to the helm in just eleven months—the period that it lasted. A group of Spanish generals then rescued the nation by establishing a constitutional monarchy and a new system was put in place called *turno pacífico* or the peaceful turn. The two parties, conservatives and liberals, now took turns in governing the nation. This was a closed political system with elections manipulated to allow the parties to alternate at regular intervals. Under this system Spain enjoyed greater prosperity than it had known in the entire 19th century.

The government defeated the Carlist insurrection and the Ten Years' War with Cuba came to an end. High tariffs protected Spanish agriculture from foreign competition, and Basque iron, steel, and manufacturing industries boomed. Madrid and Barcelona grew rapidly and installed electrical systems, telephones, electric trams, and other modern conveniences. It was also an era of cultural flowering. Barcelona became a vibrant example of avant-garde architecture; Spain's Impressionist painters, flamenco dancers and novelists achieved renown far beyond the nation's boundaries.[1] This system lasted for over two decades and was destabilized only after Spain's defeat in the Spanish–American war in 1898. Further political opening up and violent movements for democratic reforms heralded another long era of

---

1 *History of Spain*, David R Ringrose, Microsoft® Encarta® Online Encyclopedia 2009

political instability that ended with Franco's rule in 1936 that was to last 36 years.

China

China has had the rule of one party, the Chinese Communist Party (CCP), since 1949 though it has changed radically since then, especially after the market oriented economic reforms started in 1978. Since then, China has decentralized its economy but its politics remains centralized. China's biggest achievement has been drastic reduction in population below poverty line. The planning horizon is 20 years and decision making as well as execution is focused and expedient. China has invested heavily in infrastructure for the common man like roads, fresh water supply, power, drainage, and public transport. More than 6% of GDP is invested in education and a basic health care system is in place. Street crime is quite low in China as indeed is the case with most centralized states. Its response to natural calamities like the Sichuan Earthquake has been considered exemplary. China might fail on many criteria when benchmarked against the democratic developed nations, but comparing like to like, the life of an average citizen is much better in China than in any other developing country in the world today.

What are some of the key lessons from the Chinese political model? One is that implementation of party mechanisms like top leadership rotation as per a fixed term make a lot of difference. The same party was more of a dictatorship under Mao Zedong. Only after his death did the CCP reinvent itself and become a party rule in reality. Deng Xiaoping,[1] a pragmatist who was the guiding force behind China's reforms once said, "It doesn't matter whether the cat is black or white so long as it catches mice." This simple quote reflected his belief which favored pragmatism over ideology and this was to shape modern China's future. In 1980, during the Reform of Party and State leadership meeting, he said that power was over-centralized and led to archaic as well as arbitrary rule. From this point onwards, regularized and institutionalized procedures were created and rotation of top leadership terms introduced. Two offices were created, president and premier, originally meant for separation of executive and legislative pow-

---

1 Deng Xiaoping, Nation Builders, Jonathan Spence, Time, Asia, 2006, http://www.time.com/time/asia/2006/heroes/nb_deng.html

ers, with 5-year terms each with a maximum limit of two terms.[1] Further, the CCP old guard was replaced by relatively younger and better educated leaders. Deng himself had received part of his education in France, which probably influenced his pro West stance that helped China end its diplomatic isolation and integrate with the world. While having fathered such political and economic reforms, Deng did not assume any top leadership positions nor develop a cult status. The CCP now has a distinct structure and it follows set principles of internal party elections and procedures even though the power remains concentrated in the top two leaders and the CCP central committee, equivalent of a cabinet. Below the central level, party committees and congresses are formed at the provincial levels creating a large consultative participative base with about 40–60 million members, from different strata of the population. The key strength of this system has been fast decision making as well as execution and ability to focus on long term programs like investments in infrastructure and education. China has industrialized at a breathtaking speed despite the social resentment almost ubiquitous in early phases of development anywhere.

The Western nations coped through this phase relying on limited voting rights, whereas China has relied on central rule and authority. However, as it surges towards a developed nation status with a middle class majority, single party rule will become a weakness. The lack of freedom of expression and choice will become a problem as the populace climbs up the economic ladder and starts expecting fulfillment of higher order needs. But that scenario is about 20 (or more) years away.

Single party rule has been successful in many other nations too like Singapore with the People's Action Party (PAP), Mexico's Institutional Revolutionary Party (PRI), etc., with varying degrees of success. At the other end of the spectrum are nations where single party rule has devolved into cult leadership like in Cuba under Castro. Mechanisms like rotation of top leadership, fixed term concepts, and some separation of powers help it become a genuine 'party' rule.

Why does single party rule work? In most developing nations where chaos and anarchy rules and people are not ready for the birth pangs of development, centralized politics seems to hold much more promise. Deci-

---

1 Chinese Communist Party (CCP), Global security.org, 2005, http://www.globalsecurity.org/military/world/china/ccp.htm. CIA — The World Factbook, Government of China, https://www.cia.gov/library/publications/the-world-factbook/geos/ch.html

sions can be based on expert knowledge as well as longer term horizon. To go back to the beginning, an ideal state enables a good life for its citizens. Freedom to choose, have a say, and freedom to express are no doubt worthy ideals for an evolved society. But let us remind ourselves that majority of the human population lives in abject poverty, violence and misery. We should aim to first find models that fulfill their basic needs for food, water, shelter, and security before aiming for higher order needs like freedom of expression. A transient model that offers stability to these floundering nations and allows a basic level of development to take place is a prerequisite to open systems like democracy. Single party rule is one possible alternative and perhaps its most progressive form is like the *turno pacifico* system tried in Spain or the unity government in Colombia—where the two major parties of the country come together to form a unitary government and rule by turns, collaborating all the way. This is a better checked system than rule by an absolute single party as in China.

OLIGARCH REPUBLICS

While oligarchy per se means rule by a few, 'oligarch republic' here refers to democracy with limited voting rights. The Western developed nations of today started out as oligarch republics but even the ancient Greek democracy was never a mass democracy; even then voting was limited to the upper echelons of the society. In theory this should have led to an elitist rule but in reality it led to unprecedented advancement across fields like science, medicine, astronomy, philosophy, arts, and architecture. All centralized forms of rule that have been discussed are about control, law and order and good economic management in a poor country. But all of them stifle creativity, expression and innovation. Oligarch republics however seemed to marry the best of both worlds. What are the dynamics at play here?

Ancient Greece

It was in this loose collection of city states that democracy was first invented in about 500 BC. It achieved its exalted form in Athens, which is also widely considered as its birthplace. Voting rights were limited; out of a total population of about 250,000 only 30,000 male citizens had the right to vote[1]. Ancient Greece is considered as the cradle of modern Western civilization and rightly so. Early democratic tradition, trial by jury and philosophical theories were all developed in this era. Human advancement shone.[2] Pythagoras' theorem and Archimedes's principle were discovered and science and mathematics, especially geometry, evolved to a great extent. Aristarchus theorized that Earth revolved on an axis and moved around the Sun, even though this was not accepted for almost 2000 years till Copernicus proved it. Many other astronomical concepts were developed. The idea of providing formal education to children too started in these times. The Hippocratic Oath from that era continues to date. Greek architecture involved both engineering expertise and an appreciation of aesthetics. There was an evolution in both sculpture and art forms towards a naturalistic approach, a concept later revived during the Renaissance. Greek drama and theatre dealt with many themes from heroic, tragic to comic. In medicine, the role of different organs and value of many medicinal plants was studied. A lot of this knowledge was lost down the ages but sufficient survived to indicate what kind of a great era it was.

Europe

The city states of Italy about 14th century onwards too went through a similar phase though these city states were closer to oligarchies than republics. The ruling families invested heavily in patronage of arts, artists, writers and intellectuals. This led to the cultural and artistic revival now known as the Renaissance as well as the birth of Humanism. The philosophical thought process ignited during this phase with the rediscovery of ancient Greek texts, laid the foundation for the Age of Enlightenment. This was the turning point in the Western civilization that set it apart from rest of the world.

The revolution that followed in France, the nucleus of the Enlightenment Age, turned to democracy with universal voting rights and was a fail-

1   The Democratic Experiment, Paul Cartledge, Ancient History in-depth, 2009, BBC, http://www.bbc.co.uk/history/ancient/greeks/greekdemocracy_01.shtml

Democracy in Ancient Greece, Ancient Greece, http://www.ancient-greece.us/democracy.html

2   Ancient Greece, Science and Technology, Michael Lahanas, Hellenica, http://www.mlahanas.de/Greeks/Greeks.htm

ure. The turn to oligarch republics in the UK and the US and then in almost all of the developed nations of today stabilized the system.

The UK

The British society in the 19th century was becoming more fluid than in the past, in part due to the growth of the middle classes in towns and cities. Middle-class families earned their livings in trade or in professions, such as law and medicine. Increased literacy and education spread throughout the country. In towns, people established lending libraries to distribute books, clubs to discuss ideas, and coffeehouses to debate politics. Newspapers became the most popular form of media, and more than 50 towns produced their own newspapers by the end of the century[1]. Electricity, telephone, railroads, and vaccination are all contributions of this era. Not everything was positive, initially, and that bears a striking resemblance to the situation in the developing world today. Poverty dominated the lower reaches of the society, especially as the population grew and food prices rose in the middle of the century. Towns swarmed with homeless families, the sick and individuals with disabilities. The government and charitable organizations established orphanages and hospitals, as well as workhouses where the unemployed could find temporary work. Paradoxically, improvements in sanitation, medicine, and food production led to a population explosion. The epidemics of plague and smallpox, which had routinely killed a third of the people in towns during earlier centuries, were now a thing of the past. The production of cheap alcoholic beverages, such as gin and rum, eased some of the pain of the poor, but increased alcohol consumption also raised the level of violence and crime.

Things started to change after the reform bill of 1834 that extended voting rights to the middle class. The society started reforming in the direction of becoming fair to all. Britain was among the first countries to abolish slavery. One of the earliest reforms was regarding child labor starting with lesser number of working hours gradually leading up to its abolition and replacement with compulsory and free education for all children aged 5–10. Further reforms included improvements in public health, provision for safe drinking water, construction of effective sewage disposal systems etc. Social legislation aimed at improving safety and sanitary conditions in

---

1 History of the United Kingdom, Mark Kishlansky, Microsoft® Encarta® Online Encyclopedia 2009

the workplace also made headway. By the end of 19th century, living standards improved and with the spread of prosperity, the largely poor bottom end had now shrunk to a minority. The poor still exist, even in the developed world, but neither in such numbers nor nearly as miserable as in the developing world.

Whereas rule by upper class alone, as was the case with aristocracy and nobility combined, had always tended to become insensitive and self serving, extension of political rights to a prosperous middle class took a different direction. It led to a gradual awakening in the society with focus on values of thrift, education, moral behavior and sensitivity to the underprivileged. This class was able to deal with political power well without abusing it. The upper classes had failed to do so in the past and as the various democracies of the next century have shown, the predominantly poor classes do not either. The middle class provides the middling factor as had also been theorized by Aristotle. However, an oligarchy is a viable form of transitional government provided it is accompanied by "free markets" which enables the emergence of a prosperous middle class. If it were not so, power would remain concentrated in the hands of the prosperous few and would turn elitist sooner or later.

The US

The US too started with an oligarchy but one that was far more complex like the nation itself. It had two divergent branches—the North and the South. Once again, fate of democracy is largely determined by economic development preceding it. The North industrialized fast whereas the South remained agrarian and dependent on black slavery. Unlike the UK, suffrage in the US did not move in gradual step wise manner led only by economic empowerment but got hijacked by color / race issues. By 1856, all white men had the right to vote regardless of their economic status.[1] In the North, where development had preceded this, the middle class vied for equality, abolition of slavery and extension of rights to blacks. In contrast, the South that had remained agrarian and without a strong middle class that comes about through industrialization, took to brutality and self serving abuse of political power. The largely rural and poor white population opposed equality to Afro Americans in none too decent terms. Brutal lynching of

---

1 "United States History," Nancy Woloch, Paul E Johnson, Microsoft® Encarta® Online Encyclopedia 2009

blacks, prevention of laws against the same and use of threats to keep African Americans away from voting, despite having won that right in a civil war, were all too common features of this despotism.

The national government on the other hand, remained centered around the North and proceeded with caution in bringing about social changes and stayed away from entanglements in world affairs and conflicts. Freedom of press, human rights, trial by jury and so forth. gave a new meaning to an average citizen's life. The state power was sufficiently checked and it existed to serve the ruled than the rulers. America industrialized faster than any other nation and faced the same challenges initially as the UK, namely child labor, urban squalor, the tendency of the rich to get richer and the poor poorer, etc. but the oligarch government was able to push through the development agenda. It thus laid the foundation of an industrial economy that was to make the US the greatest economic superpower a century later.

Republics with limited suffrage or right to vote have been the precursors of most successful democracies of our time. The model was greatly successful not only in helping the respective nations along the development path but also in great bursts of innovations in all fields. Widely divergent political concepts were debated, politics was dominated by ideologues and it was an era of great intellectual advancement. Oligarchy as a transient governance model stabilized these societies and actually helped bring about stable and progressive democracies later on. But the road from oligarchy to democracy was long and arduous stretching over a century or two. Autocracy to oligarchy to democracy ought to have been the right transition. Developing world could have gone this way too but for early nations like India where limited suffrage was debated[1] but forsaken in the idealistic zeal. After that no nation has even considered anything other than universal suffrage. For nations achieving independence after World War II the end result looked attractive but they did not understand the essential processes of making a successful democracy any more than it is understood even today. Typically, leaders of newly independent nations would visit the Western countries, like what they see there—widespread prosperity and respect for human rights. They would ascribe it fully to democracy, come back and implement it in their own countries in all earnestness, yet the results would turn out markedly different from what they, as well as rest of the world, expected. It may be

---

1 India after Gandhi – The history of the world's largest democracy, Ramachandra Guha, (Picador India, 2007)

safe to conclude at this stage that we haven't quite understood the political dynamics in the developing countries so far. Let us attempt that.

CHAPTER 4. WOOING THE VOTERS: RULES OF THE GAME

A government "by the people and of the people" should quite naturally deliver ideal governance "for the people." But in reality it does not. While it starts with this simple motto of people power, it soon meanders its way into a more complex terrain. A basic problem with democracy is that voters do not make rational or truly informed choices. Their political decision making seems to be driven by emotional criteria plus they have a bias for instant gratification thus keeping most democracies focused on the short term. Freebies, divide and rule, candidates' X factor and smear campaigns have a large bearing on the voters' decisions. Long term programs like infrastructure creation and investment in education are hard tasks where benefits come with a time lag and entails a possibility that the one who sows is unlikely to also be the one who reaps. Politicians shy away from such selfless agendas. Emptying the exchequer and giving short term freebies or using a divide and rule strategy has immediate returns with a surer shot at winning elections. The resultant governance in essence is an embodiment of electoral preferences and politicians ability to maneuver around these tendencies. "Elections," the fundamental process of a democracy, ironically, are the starting point for most of its troubles. Unearthing electoral erroneous zones is the first step to understanding what changes are necessary to move democracy closer to its end goal of good governance as delivered. Let us step into the murky world of elections and see what the rules of winning this game are.

INSTANT GRATIFICATION—RULE BY FREEBIES

In most developing world democracies, there is a trend of doling out freebies to voters in cash or kind in the run up to elections. The growing power of such schemes is a result of their apparent success in garnering votes. How do these schemes impact the exchequer as well as the development program of a nation? Let us examine through a few examples.

India—The Tamil Nadu TV scheme

Distribution of freebies in election or pre-election years is a deeply ingrained tradition in democratic India. This often takes the form of cash bribes, free rice, saris, or loan waivers and by now is almost a mandatory part of all election campaigns. One of the southern states, Tamil Nadu (TN), however, took the game to an altogether new level. Prior to the 2006 assembly elections, a leading party, DMK, made the usual promises of 2kg bags of rice, saris, and land to the landless peasants. The same or similar promises were also made by its rival, AIADMK, the ruling party at the time. DMK then tried an innovative scheme to break through the clutter. It promised distribution of free color TV sets to all poor homes in the state. The scheme was an instant hit with the voters and probably a large contributor to the party's success in the ensuing elections. Skeptics doubted the government would make good on a seemingly ridiculous idea but that was not the case. In all earnestness, once in power, DMK started distributing color TV sets[1]. Elaborate functions would be held where some party leader would personally distribute the sets to people who turned up with an ID card. "Benefits for the poor" was just an excuse to make it sound politically correct, as often people even came in cars to collect their free TVs, probably an additional set in the house. However, the lack of access to fresh drinking water has been one of the biggest problems facing this state. In many a village, while distributing TV sets, the party dignitaries often made promises of someday also bringing roads and fresh water; however, color TV is here and now. For instance, in Tiruvannamalai district, over 0.4 million families received free

---

1 "Eat more, Watch TV, Procreate," T R Vivek, Mar 29, 2006, *Outlook India*, http://www.outlookindia.com/article.aspx?230719

color TVs, costing the exchequer about $22 million, while a fraction of that, a mere $0.5 million, was allotted to alleviating the district's water problem[1].

About 9 million TV sets have been distributed in the state and plans are afoot for millions more. The average penetration of color TVs in India is around 27 per cent whereas TN was already higher at 30 per cent; soon it might be universal. The scheme has been a resounding success with the electorate and led the party to a thumping win in the 2009 elections.

All this while, the state continues to operate with a deficit budget and has a ballooning debt which has grown by 19% in one year and stands at about $19 billion in 2010. Contrary to attempting any austerity measures, many more funds disbursement schemes[2] have been announced in the 2010–11 budget.

While the opposition has claimed extravagant spending on color TVs to be the cause of the state's growing deficit and debt problem, that part of the objection isn't entirely true. It does not cost all that much at the end of the day, adding up to around $1 billion for the entire scheme[3], just about 5% of the state debt. True development initiatives like building roads and getting fresh water to villages would cost hundreds of times more for even a small district. The process would be slow and the impact not really felt. From the voters' perspective, the color TV set really feels like the government gave something concrete to them and seems to show that the party cares for them and hence must be voted for. The party's huge popularity also insulates it from prosecution for illegal acts. In 2007, a press office was burnt down, killing staff members over a petty dispute with one of Chief Minister's sons. In 2009, all accused were acquitted[4] and walked free. Journalists at times have been attacked for just covering any peaceful demonstration against the chief minister. So long as you can bribe the voters, despotism or economic mismanagement is forgiven.

---

1 Rs 2 crore for Drinking Water problem, Tiruvannamalai, Apr 26, 2010, *The Hindu*, http://beta.thehindu.com/news/cities/Chennai/article410238.ece?service=mobile

2 Karunanidhi launches Phase 3 of CTV, gas stove scheme, Chennaionline, Feb 17, 2008, http://news.chennaionline.com/newsitem.aspx?NEWSID=7b4c8591-621f-44c6-afda-075bb5c8c991&CATEGORYNAME=CHN

3 Approximation based on : Tamil Nadu to Source 4 Million Color TVs for Rs. 8.24 billion, 16 Dec 2009, LankaNewspapers.com, http://www.lankanewspapers.com/news/2009/12/51431_space.html

4 Acquittal for all accused in Dinakaran office burning case, Dec 10, 2009, Zee News, http://www.zeenews.com/news586176.html

Compare this to the alternate development route. In a state where fresh water is scarce, if the state were to focus on supplying fresh drinking water to the poor or expanding the primary education network, it would take a budget many times greater, a lot of toil and sweat, and, no doubt, operationally the corrupt state machinery would have to gear up to deliver. Emptying the exchequer and distributing such a novelty item to the populace seems like a lucrative alternative to genuine development. However, another 50 or even 100 years down the line, the state will continue to struggle with basic problems like scarcity of fresh drinking water, roads, and schools. But the voters can forget their worries and watch cable TV instead.

The state deserves an accolade for making a total mockery of the concept of democracy and elections. But it is not alone in following this strategy of freebies; most Indian states as well as national parties engage in all forms of bribery starting from cash distribution to loan waivers, free electrical power etc., in the run up to election years[1]. Voters understand and appreciate such bribes and are only too willing to sell out. As a trade off, the much needed investments in infrastructure and education lag far behind (since that requires intense efforts, huge budgets and takes a long time before the effects are felt by the common man). India has a small base of income tax payers, a mere 31.5 million[2] in a population of 1.2 billion, out of which 700 million are the registered voters[3]. Since the majority does not pay an income tax, it does not "feel" that what the government is doling out to them is their own money. In the end they do pay for it either through tariffs or through the "hidden tax" of inflation. But that reality is too hard for them to grasp and elections are a game of "perceptions." A party that gives them something free, over and above the bribes being offered by other parties, wins this perception game. India is a long-running democracy and such evolved election stunts have become second nature. But others are not far behind and learning the ropes rather quickly.

---

1 Indians Vote for Dal-Roti, Ignore Stability, Devinder Sharma, 24 May 2009, Dawn. com, http://www.dawn.com/wps/wcm/connect/dawn-content-library/dawn/ in-paper-magazine/encounter/indians-vote-for-dalroti-ignore-stability-459

2 "India has 31.5 Million Tax Payers," 28 Jul 2007, *The Economic Times*, http://economic-times.indiatimes.com/India_has_315_million_taxpayers/articleshow/2240281.cms

3 Drawing a comparison with a developed nation like US, there are 138 million tax payers in a population of 310 million out of which 169 million are the registered voters.

Cash and Other Bribes

In Kenya, the 2007 elections were a telling point for its democracy. Not only the election violence was of an unprecedented scale, its parties also spent millions of dollars bribing the voters. The Coalition for Accountable Party Finance estimated that out of the $90 million fund raised by the parties, about 40% was used as bribes[1]. Allegations relate to both the leading parties, ODM as well as PNU. The report insists several government departments like the state owned Electricity Company overcharged customers and donated the surplus to the political parties. In the 2006 elections in Mexico, an estimated 4 million voters were paid cash bribes to vote for a party. This was done by most of the parties. Some rural voters were paid $40–$60 per vote, a neat sum in a country where the poor families subsist on less than $4 a day[2]. Voters were asked to take a picture of their ballot with their cell phone cameras to validate their payment. In Venezuela, a massive food distribution program was launched with a lot of fanfare by Hugo Chavez with the opening of communal soup pots. Just a few years down the line, the nation is facing food shortages as well as an inflation rate higher than that in the rest of Latin America. Investigations also revealed that the voters were bribed with cash, food and even blenders to vote for Chavez in the 2008 elections[3]. In Egypt, which is not a democracy, such freebies are distributed by the Muslim brotherhood. People hail them as pro poor (especially vis-à-vis the government) but do not realize that the Brotherhood does not have to provide roads, electricity, water and other infrastructure services which come at a monumental cost but are taken for granted.

This kind of exploitation of freebies and bribing voters with short term measures has become the first commandment of winning elections in the developing world. Such initiatives are also hailed by activists as they do benefit the poor. But poverty has a root cause which needs to be addressed; just giving relief measures is only treating the symptoms not the disease itself. Poverty alleviation requires employment creation which in

---

1 Kenya's Parties 'Bribed Voters', BBC News, 25 Apr 2008, http://news.bbc.co.uk/2/hi/africa/7367008.stm

2 "Dirty politics 'ingrained' in Mexico," Manuel Roig-Franzia, 26 June 2006, *The Washington Post*, http://www.washingtonpost.com/wp-dyn/content/article/2006/06/25/AR2006062500790.html

3 "Chavez government handed out millions in exchange for votes," 2008, *El Nuevo Herald*, http://worldnews.about.com/od/venezuela/tp/venezuelanews.htm

turn needs investment in infrastructure, education as well as stimulation of the economy. While a voter understands when a dignitary comes and hands him a free color TV set or a bowl of soup, he is unable to appreciate the "invisible hand" of the government in a vibrant economy. If employment opportunities are created, he feels he worked hard to earn the salary; what did the government do? But if he gets something free he feels ingratiated to the party or the leader. The issue here is not morality of politicians but voters' inability to discriminate between a bribe and development. This does lead to short term oriented governance where investment needs of a nation are forsaken in favor of short term relief measures. Ideally there should be a balance between short and long term programs but voters' perceptions of "what is good for them" drive it largely in favor of the former. Valuable resources are diverted from essential development projects to gratifying or bribing the voters instantly. Investment in education and infrastructure is dwindling as it is resource consuming yet not trusted by voters who dismiss it as empty promises or even pro rich strategies. Ultimately the system becomes what it rewards.

While every fallacy of democracy is magnified many times over in the developing world, the developed world is not immune to this strategy either. Sweden is often considered a model state for balancing market dynamics with welfare measures. Sweden went through an economic crisis in the early 1990s, quite similar to the one faced by most of the world in the late 2000s. It managed the economic reforms and consolidation in an exemplary manner keeping all sections of the society in focus and without losing sight of the long term goals. The economy rebounded in record time and Sweden actually came back stronger post the crisis. It has also received its due accolades from experts, who have hailed it as a role model for rest of the world especially in the ongoing crisis. How was this turnaround achieved? More importantly, what was the political fallout for the miracle men and party who achieved it?

Sweden

Sweden turned to universal suffrage democracy in 1921 and the Social Democratic Party (SDP) ruled the nation for almost an unbroken spell till 1991, in varying coalitions with other parties. Since the beginning of the 20th century, Sweden geared itself towards a mixed economy and its welfare program kept expanding. By about 1960s, it provided for education, health care, pensions, childcare, and unemployment benefits. The extensive welfare program peaked about the 1970s. This helped the SDP consolidate its image and the party kept growing from strength to strength in popularity and elections. Then, in the 1980s, a housing and financial bubble formed in Sweden which burst in the early 1990s[1]. Sweden faced a financial crisis similar to the one later faced by most of the developed world post 2007.

Between 1990 and 1993, GDP went down, unemployment skyrocketed, the banking sector faced a potential meltdown and there was a run on the currency. Sweden made swift moves to bail out the banking sector and arrested a potential collapse. However, the welfare system that had been growing rapidly for decades couldn't be sustained with a falling GDP, lower employment and larger welfare payments. Coinciding with the turmoil, the SDP had a poor showing in the 1991 elections and it lost power to the Moderate Party. But voters were quick to come back to the SDP in the 1994 elections and the party returned to the seat of power.

Budgetary discipline and economic reforms seemed imminent and the SDP led government acted with alacrity. Finance Minister Göran Persson presented a budgetary consolidation plan which was approved by the parliament. Transparency was a key aspect of the plan. Instead of the usual empty promises and emotional rhetoric of hope and optimism that politicians engage in, the gravity of the debt crisis was emphasized to all stakeholders alike, and it was well understood. Being in debt means being not free! Power shifts from people's representatives to lenders—be it lending countries or financial markets. That would undermine democracy and people's confidence in the political system. This moral dimension of the crisis was borne in mind. An advertisement at the time showed the picture of a new-born baby with the caption, "Born with a debt of 150,000 Swedish Kronor."

Consolidation was also designed as a package to not single out any losers. Cuts in pensions were matched by cuts in child benefits and unemployment insurance and bundled together with an increase in income taxes for the richest[2]. This infused some sense of fairness into the painful but un-

---

1 Structural Problems and Reforms, Swedish Economic History, © Ekonomifakta 2010, http://www.ekonomifakta.se/en/Swedish-economic-history/Structural-Problems-and-Reforms/

2 Sweden has one of the highest income tax rates in the world with the upper bracket being 60%. At the lower end, people find it more profitable to be unemployed and take the associated benefits than to get a job and pay high taxes. This

avoidable exercise of cuts in benefits. One of the most crucial aspects of the plan was commitment to long term societal goals even amidst crisis. One area that was avoided in the cuts was investments especially in education. The argument was that as an adult you could always live with having had an economically poor childhood but it is much harder to compensate for poor education[1]. In fact post consolidation also Sweden invested heavily in higher education, thus opening up economic opportunities in the IT arena in the ensuing decade. The Swedish politicians also made personal commitments by putting their jobs on the line and stuck to the plan. The progress was shared in a transparent manner with the citizens and the financial markets. This swift and focused implementation led to a quick economic recovery.

In 1994, Sweden had turned into a deficit economy with its budgetary deficit at 15% and debt at 74% of the GDP, well above the 3% and 60% respective limits set by the EU. Barely four years into the crisis, the huge budget deficit turned into a surplus and remained that way for the years to come. GDP started growing again at about 4%, well above the European average and inflation came down. The government steadily brought the debt down to 37% of GDP by 2007. All in all, it was an unprecedented swift and sustained recovery which till date is touted as one of the best examples[2] of financial crisis management.

Had Sweden not undertaken this exercise, it would have lost out economically and its welfare system would have become unsustainable. Instead Sweden upheld its egalitarian principles through a more rational system while maintaining a globally competitive economy.

Perhaps no people can ask more of their politicians. So, what was the political fallout for SDP out of this?

While the economy has had a strong showing, the SDP has gradually lost power as the base of voters whose benefits were rationalized, have simply turned away. In 1994, when the economy was in a worsening crisis, the SDP was voted into power with a resounding 45% of votes. As the budgetary consolidation plan was put into place, this vote share fell sharply to 36%

---

disincentive to work is recognized by most European parties but they do not have a clear path to dismantling it.

1   Ten lessons about Budget Consolidation, Jens Henriksson, © Bruegel 2007, http:// www.bruegel.org/uploads/tx_btbbreugel/el_010607_budget.pdf

2   Japan, Sweden may offer Economic Recovery lessons, Manav Tanneeru, 2 Apr 2009, CNN International, http://edition.cnn.com/2009/US/04/02/japan.sweden/ index.html

in the 1998 elections. Seeing this as an opportunity, the right wing made an appeal for dismantling the welfare model which backfired and briefly brought voters back to the SDP in 2002. But the Alliance for Sweden soon learnt and realigned its strategy to the center and ran a negative campaign against the SDP's indifference to voters with rising unemployment in the 2006 elections. It won the elections as the SDP received only 32% of votes, its poorest showing yet since 1921. In reality, economic growth was strong at 4.1%, inflation low and even more importantly, unemployment, made out to be a big election issue was just about 5%. Yet the SDP's indifference, as projected by opposition, resonated with the voters whose direct free benefits had been cut. As a result, 2006 was an electoral disaster for the SDP forcing the leader, Persson, the architect of the most acclaimed budgetary consolidation plan, to resign as the party leader. In 2007, he also announced his resignation from the *Riksdag* where he had served 1979–1985 and from 1991 till 2007.

Overall, SDP followed a long term approach of stabilizing the banking system, balancing the budget without cuts in investments and stimulating the economy. It couldn't have been more prudent. But the voters were not able to understand or appreciate this complex management of economy despite evidence of good showing. They only understood the direct free benefits that had come down for them. Elections are a game of perceptions. Voters were unable to perceive the government's "invisible hand" in the strong economic performance. Nor did they appreciate the investment in education and training as these bear results in the longer term. But getting something free or losing a benefit is instant and concrete. It resonated far more sharply in their minds and the SDP, once considered the strongest party in all of Europe, is on a steep decline[1]. In 2006 elections, the SDP had its poorest showing yet since 1921.

In Germany the Social Democrats suffered a similar fate in the 2000s. SPD leader Gerhard Schröder formed a government in alliance with the Greens in 1998, positioning himself as a centrist candidate. He went on to win a second term post the 2002 elections. In 2003, he announced a program of economic reforms, called Agenda 2010. It rationalized some of the unemployment benefits and created subsidies for unemployed people who

---

1 "The rise and fall of the 'Swedish Model" 10 Nov 2009, *Socialist Party*, http://www. socialistparty.net/international/282-is-sweden-socialist-the-rise-and-fall-of-the-qswedish-modelq

start their own business. This sparked protests and the SDP started to lose popularity in some of its heartland provinces, pressurizing Schröder to call for early elections in 2005, which he lost[1]. This is often considered as the time when the SDP base started to shrink in Germany and it did even worse in the 2009 elections. All the same, Schröder's reforms are largely credited with the economic upswing and fall in unemployment in Germany after 2006/2007. The plan was a long term initiative and was successful in meeting many of its objectives. However the champion of reforms was not there to reap the benefits nor was the electorate aware of its folly as the SDP's base continues to shrink.

Needless to say, this does not augur well for democracies which are increasingly turning myopic. What voters reward is what the governments will gravitate towards delivering. It is no surprise then that most governments are running up huge deficits, leaving the worries of ballooning debt to the next ones. They are wary of announcing much needed austerity measures and delay them as long as possible, usually until it the crisis can no longer be avoided. In the *Gorgias*, Socrates argued that his trial would be like a doctor prosecuted by a cook who asks a jury of children to choose between the doctor's bitter medicine and the cook's tasty treats. Maybe there is a parallel here with modern democratic elections. Ideally, a nation ought to strike a balance between short and long term, between benefits and investments. But while no one reacts when there is not enough being invested, any cuts or consolidation of benefits has a negative political fallout. As Jens Henriksson[2] points out in his analysis of Sweden's budgetary consolidation, the media has another perspective—"If you cut down on child benefit, they will run a story on a mother of seven. If you raise real estate tax, it will be about old people that will have to move since they can no longer afford to live in the house they built with their very own hands." He further believes that a cynical mind could draw the following lesson from Sweden's example—if you have to consolidate, wait for a deep crisis to occur. Since there is no alternative but to fix the deficit, people may blame you less for your actions. So it would be easy to do, easy to communicate and easy to be re-elected afterwards. Sweden's conscientious political leadership dismissed this cynical view and instead followed a prudent approach and the

---

1 "Germany takes its medicine badly," David Lawday, 5 Apr 2004, *New Statesman*, http://www.newstatesman.com/200404050021

2 Ten lessons about Budget Consolidation, Jens Henriksson, © Bruegel 2007, http://www.bruegel.org/uploads/tx_btbbreugel/el_010607_budget.pdf

voters punished them for it. What is the motivation for politicians to follow Sweden's example? No doubt: they aren't following it.

USE OF RELIGION—HOW FAITH SEALS AND STEALS THE BALLOT

If giving voters instant gratification is the first commandment of democracy, rabble rousing them through religion and religion-inspired conservatism is the second. Religion's role in politics has always been a point of contention even in the pre modern times when aristocratic empires ruled the world and were in constant conflict with the power of religious bodies. In democracies of our time, religion has been a predominant divisive factor often sparking violence and insurgency. While it has played a most destabilizing and divisive role in the developing world, religion's return to politics in the developed world as a recent trend deserves mention first.

The United States

During the Middle Ages, the Church dominated the society as well as the intellectual thought processes in the West. The Scientific Revolution as well as the Age of Enlightenment challenged that and brought about a separation of state and religion. Most of the revolutionaries were believers, themselves, but advocated separation of state and religion. The US constitution incorporates the principles of secularity and religious freedom, although in very broad terms. Even though the religion of a candidate has been known to influence voters' choices, it was never recognized as a central force in the US politics. It was a fringe issue in the 2000 elections that were given to George W. Bush, but by 2004 it had been made into a central force.

One step in bringing religion to the fore was a seemingly innocuous prayer meeting in the White House with religious leaders to seek a spiritual answer to why 9/11 had happened. Perhaps every American was asking that question. Soon, a White House office of "faith-based initiatives" was established to offer free grants to religious bodies. Slowly, the party inspired discussion of socio-religious issues. There were heated debates on opposition to stem cell research, abortion and gay marriages. To cap it all, the US started turning the clock back to challenge the theory of evolution and going back to Christian creationism to explain human genesis. Thus slowly and steadily the Bush era brought religion into the center stage of

American politics. Critics panned it as undermining the American founding principles of separation of church and state but people were divided over how much role religion should play in politics[1]. Let us examine the impact of mixing religion with politics.

In 2000, the US had a surplus economy. The previous government had worked hard to balance the budget by both increasing receipts and lowering expenditures. But by 2004, the US had been turned into a deficit economy and started to have a year on year ballooning debt problem. A costly war had been waged on Iraq based on false information. International institutions like the UN had been reviled and put into an irrelevant corner and cronyism became the new norm for pushing through interventionist agenda. The US image took a battering the world over and the nation lost all the sympathy it had gained post 9/11. Despite having a defense budge larger than rest of the world's put together, the man blamed for September 11, Osama Bin Laden, remained at large while Bush pursued an anti-Saddam drive in Iraq. Budget outlays were increasing but there were no major increases in social benefits for the average citizen. To the contrary, as US debt mounted, a large portion of its funding came from social security, which is money invested by citizens to be en-cashed when they retire. While America passionately debated stem cell research, gay marriages, abortion and religious creationism, its social security network was being stolen by the government to fund costly wars and unexplained expenditures.

By any token of imagination with such performance, no president who had been in office should have continued into a second term. That is what democracy is all about—accountability, which means being accountable to the electorate. A leader comes to power on certain promises and then delivers national governance. If he takes a nation downhill, democracy should be expected to replace him. But that did not happen as elections were hijacked by manipulative, divisive tactics like religion, which shifted focus away from actual governance to emotional issues. Religion and associated social issues became a powerful smokescreen in the 2004 elections. A stealth campaign was run by the religious right (that Bush had ardently cultivated) and he won the election, although by a thin margin. As the Fourth National Survey of Religion and Politics revealed, his support came from traditionalist elements across Christian sects. The survey revealed that social issue priori-

---

1 More Americans question religion's role in politics, 21 Apr 2008, The Pew Forum on religion and public life, http://pewforum.org/PublicationPage.aspx?id=1028

ties were most important to Bush's constituencies.[1] In contrast, economic issues were most important to his rival, Kerry's constituencies. Religion had clearly swung the election. But even so, he only managed to scrape through the election with a thin margin. In a developing country, hypothetically, he would likely have won a landslide victory. We'll understand more of that later.

Anyhow, the US government continued with more of the same governance that had won it the second term. As if people were oblivious to the looming economic crisis, debates on social and religious issues continued to dominate American politics. In 2003 itself the debt had crossed the 60% of GDP benchmark; it continued rising, becoming 70% of GDP by 2008. As Sweden had verbalized, being in debt means being not free; the power shifts from people's representatives to the lenders. The biggest lenders to the US now emerged from the East, like Japan, China and proxy companies funded by the oil bloc nations.

Bush's second term was a mirror image of his first. If the government had been held accountable on rational criteria, he should not have won a second term and the damage would have been controlled. But religion tends to cloud people's judgment, and thus can be used as a manipulative tool. An election can easily be hijacked by religious and associated moral preaching as a neat cover up for political and economic mismanagement. Even future candidates could rise to power using the easy route of religious conservatism and rabble rousing while lacking in any distinct political or economic ideology. The use of religion in politics stands to threaten accountability in a democracy.

In the developing world, religious intervention in democracy politics has led to more disastrous results. It has often resulted in communal violence, riots, genocides, militancy, terrorism as well as persecution of progressives. This has happened in several countries across Asia, Africa etc. and constantly makes headlines. Let us look at two examples where extra democratic factors have tried to curb religious intervention in politics.

---

1 Religion and the 2004 Election: A Pre Election Analysis, John C Green, The Pew Forum, http://pewforum.org/uploadedfiles/Topics/Issues/Politics_and_Elections/green-full.pdf

Turkey

Mustafa Kemal Atatürk founded the modern Turkish republic in 1923 and ruled the nation until his death in 1938. His modern secular principles, often known as *Kemalism*, became a guiding force in shaping the nation. After World War II, Turkey became a democratic republic. In line with *Kemalism*, its constitution incorporated a ban on headscarves in public offices, ceremonies and universities as they were regarded as a challenge to the secular nature of Turkey. Since the 1950s, religious sentiment has at times intermingled with politics. The military has intervened in the political process on a few occasions whenever it feared that political parties posed a threat to the secular nature of the state, a principle it holds as sacrosanct in line with Turkey's constitution. In such cases, the matter is handed over to the constitutional court which bans religious-leaning parties altogether and bars their leaders from politics for 5 years. Let us see how democracy operates under such constraints.

Turkey saw the rise of Islamist parties like Refah and Virtue in the 1980s and the 1990s. But they were banned by the constitutional court on grounds of threat to secularism. The moderates in these parties then reconstituted themselves as a new party, the Justice and Development Party (AKP). As before, any religious leaning parties were an instant hit with the voters and the AKP won the 2001 elections. While AKP leadership denies it, the party is accused of having a stealth Islamic agenda. The Majority of AKP deputies and their family members wear their faith on their sleeve, which is asserted to have helped the party's popularity immensely.[1]

Initially the AKP was even able to win some of the conservative Kurdish vote bloc by appealing to a sense of Muslim solidarity, though later these groups felt alienated. After the AKP's attempt to lift the headscarf ban, the courts first warned and then started legal proceedings to close down the party, saying "it has become a hotbed of anti secularist activities"—which is against the Turkish constitution. After deliberating for 3 days the court gave its verdict in July 2008. The AKP was found guilty of becoming the focus of anti secularist actions. A qualified majority of 7 out of 11 votes is required to disband a political party. But only 6 members of the court voted

---

1 Turkey's transformation under AKP-I: Rise and demise of moderate Islamism, Soner Çağaptay, 4 Apr 2010, Hurriyet Daily News, http://www.hurriyetdailynews. com/n.php?n=turkey8217s-transformation-under-akp-i-the-rise-and-demise-of-moderate-islamism-2010-04-02

in favor of disbanding the party, thus falling short of the required qualified majority by one vote.[1]

Perhaps owing to such measures, the AKP did not swing to the religious right and its leadership remained with a progressive conservative, Erdoğan, and did not devolve to the radicals. He focused on Turkey's economy and undertook several reforms which were successful. The AKP's first term was hailed as one of the better managed eras for the Turkish economy. But the global economic crisis has also hit Turkey. Since 2009, unemployment and inflation have risen while the nation, like most in the world today also struggles against a debt problem. The AKP, at the same time, has been criticized for being authoritarian and intolerant of criticism.[2] Freedom of expression has seen a decline in Turkey in the AKP era and intellectuals like Orhan Pamuk have faced considerable threats. Hrant Dink, a leading secular voice of the Armenian minorities, was assassinated during these increasingly intolerant times.

The AKP won the 2007 elections in a landslide victory while the CHP, the *Kemalist* party, remained stable at about 20%, which is roughly the proportion of secularists in Turkey. Despite the recent economic downturn, the party remains strong since as of now it is the only religious leaning party. But it is also believed that the AKP could become so strong that it could even rewrite the constitution. If that were brought about, such amendments would help the party strengthen its hold vis-à-vis the *Kemalists*, but it would no doubt also open the doors to political competition from other religious leaning parties with perhaps greater radical leadership. It remains to be seen how this unfolds.

Algeria

Post independence from French rule in 1962, Algeria turned to democracy which bred a fair degree of chaos and disorder, prompting a military takeover. The nation was secular and stable during this period. In the 1980s, economic decline led to protests and pressure for democracy. Bowing to these demands, the military regime revised the constitution in 1989, allow-

---

1 Turkey's ruling party escapes ban, 30 Jul 2008, BBC News, http://news.bbc. co.uk/2/hi/europe/7533414.stm

2 Turkey: AKP pays the price, Gareth Jenkins, 1 Apr 2009, ISN ETH Zurich, International Relations and Security Network, http://www.isn.ethz.ch/isn/ Current-Affairs/Security-Watch/Detail/?lng=en&id=98450

ing a multi party democratic system, and prepared for elections.[1] Immediately upon the advent of democracy, the Islamic Salvation Front (FIS) rose to prominence. In the 1990 provincial election, the FIS defeated the military backed party by an overwhelming margin. Rescheduled parliamentary elections held in 1992 were cancelled as the first round of balloting made it likely that the Islamists would win control of the parliament. While the military was ready to give up power, it did not want religious elements to take over the nation. This led to an armed conflict between the government forces and Islamic militants which claimed more than 100,000 lives. The militants targeted members of military and government officials as well as individuals expressing secular or non Muslim views including journalists, teachers, writers, intellectuals, foreigners and both Muslim and Christian clerics. In the wake of such religious hijacking of the national politics, the Algerian constitution was revised in 1996. Most notably, it banned political parties based exclusively on religion, language, race, gender or region. Any form of political association was disallowed if based on any of these divisive elements. More than 40 parties are active in Algeria, which shows that the military accepts opposition and a multi party democracy but not a theocracy, even through the mechanism of democracy. An amnesty in 1999 led many rebels to lay down their arms but sporadic violence has continued, even escalating post 2006.

The issue here is not about what role should religion play in people's lives or a society but only its role in politics. Not just in the nations highlighted above but in most of the developing world, where the population base is largely poor, rural and conservative, any party espousing a religious program is a sure election winner. Instead of working on political and economic ideologies for years to establish a new political party, identifying with a religious agenda leads them to an outright and instant victory. They don't seem to lose support even in an economic downturn since people are loyal to such parties, often confusing them with their faith. Such a party can only be defeated by another religious-leaning party and perhaps a more radical one. It is also noteworthy that such parties are never able to win votes with their urban educated progressive classes. These are no doubt the more "discerning voters," harder to rabble rouse or sway through non governance issues. This segment had already formed a majority in the Western world before the advent of universal suffrage democracy. But in the develop-

---

1 History of Algeria, Microsoft® Encarta® Online Encyclopedia 2009

ing world they still form a minority whereas power prematurely has been placed in the hands of the as yet poor, rural and conservative majority.

It is imperative to understand that when a political leader espouses a religious program, it becomes hard for people to question that, as it is tantamount to questioning their faith. This ensures electoral victory but since it is on a non governance related issue, it removes accountability in a democracy. This is not a comment on the role religion should play in a society or people's lives. But religion should be barred from intermingling with politics, as was done in Algeria through the constitutional amendment, thereby limiting religion's role to the "spiritual domain", which is where it is meant to be. In political power games it can be used to hijack a ballot and make a mockery of democracy.

OTHER DIVISIVE FACTORS

In most developing world democracies, elections revolve around some kind of divisive factor. Most nations are heterogeneous with presence of diverse groups split along regions, religions, sects, sub sects, languages, ethnicity or castes. Usually, these naturally existing divisions are the easiest dimensions to exploit in politics. Developing ideological differentiation in politics is a tough task as evolved political dialogue is hard to convey to a vastly poor class. But exciting them along sectarian lines is easy and has today become a fundamental building block of democracy in the developing world.

India—Vote Your Caste

India has a rudimentary caste system where people are divided into a social hierarchy. The supposedly lowest caste, now called the *dalits*, comprising about 16–20% of the population, suffer a particularly severe form of exploitation, violence and apartheid[1].

While this continues unabated in rural India, in urban sprawling metropolises its effect has started to wane. A reason for that perhaps is that caste, unlike race or color, is not easily identifiable by looking at a person. There are thousands of family names divided into vague clusters. In a small village setting with little mobility, these divisions remained historical and

---

1 Plight of Rural Dalit Women in India: A Sociological Analysis, Rajendra Prasad Jaiswal, Mahatma Gandhi Kashi Vidyapith, womensglobalconnection.org

rigid. But in large cities with diverse populations and fast-changing lives, caste-based discrimination had waned across the nation and all but disappeared in many of the large cities. However in the 1990s, it made a comeback through the process of democracy and has now become a predominant divisive factor in rural as well as urban India. Parties and candidates align themselves with various caste blocs, campaign along such divisive lines and even the media reports all election results by caste segments.[1]

Further, while there was clarity of lowest and upper castes, most of the middle band was a nebulous area. Political opportunists decided to target the middle majority and created an artificial new caste bloc called OBC—other backward castes. Since it is an artificial and politically inspired division, often there is confusion as to who can classify under it. In Rajasthan state, two rival groups, Meena and Gujjars engaged in a violent conflict with demands for their inclusion in the OBC category and exclusion of the other. While special reservations in jobs etc. had been there for *dalits* too, no one had ever wanted their caste to be included among *dalits* because it brings social discrimination and oppression with it. In case of OBCs, which is just an artificial category without any attendant oppression or discrimination, people are clashing to get included in it. To explain it in simple terms, the way this division was created was, let us say, a survey is done in an area and it emerges that the Peters are slightly better off than the Pauls. All the Pauls thereafter are declared backward and affirmative action is initiated in their favor. Thus while no noticeable overt discrimination existed between similar caste segments, randomly occurring differences in the population were used by political opportunists to divide the society. Special freebies and job reservations are offered to this new OBC segment to lure their vote. At the same time, OBCs form the predominant segment that commits atrocities on the lowest strata of *dalits*. They have been implicated in most land grabbing cases in UP, a north Indian state. In another state, Khairlanji village, lynching is one notorious example of this kind of oppression where men and women of the OBC majority brutally tortured and killed a *dalit* family for daring to send their children to school as well as protesting against land grabbing[2]. But being carved out of the middle majority, they have become

---

1 "Caste Politics in India, 'resurgence of caste politics' in contemporary India," Aditya Nigam, *South Asian Journal*, Apr–Jun 2004, http://www.southasianmedia.net/Magazine/Journal/castepolitics_india.htm
2 UP tops in crimes against *dalits*, majority of land grabbing cases by OBCs, 7 Nov 2006, IBN Live, http://ibnlive.in.com/news/up-tops-in-crimes-against-

the most critical vote bloc and are promised every possible benefit, like extensive reservations in jobs, educational institutes, etc. A majority bloc thus corners the meager resources of the nation through the process of democracy, while also continuing oppression of the lower minority castes. Further data shows that the OBC category is better off than many other population segments that do not have similar benefits.

Caste based segregation and oppression continues to be a serious ill. In urban India, it is done more covertly. The supposedly upper caste, *Brahmins*, continue to enjoy higher educational and professional status. Despite benefiting from India's accessible higher education, a section of this class uses their "higher educated" status to further assert their caste superiority rather than challenge the system. Amidst such indifference, "supposedly" lowest caste *dalits* continue to be India's most oppressed segment. Since independence, they have been granted reservations in jobs and education but as most of them are illiterate they cannot avail of this affirmative action. Plus their problem continues to be apartheid and violence committed against them in the vast rural hinterland where law and order is almost nonexistent. Even so, their lot improved slightly since 1991 post the economic reforms. Development and urbanization seem to be the right solutions to this long standing ill in the Indian rural society. But that remains stalled, again on account of democracy.

India is also divided along regional, linguistic and religious lines. In search of jobs people have moved to large cities where all these divisions have come down. Urbanization thus has been a harmonizing factor in India. But harmony stands threatened as divisive caste politics has started to permeate democracy at all levels now, including the hitherto progressive urban India.

Iraq

Post overthrow of the Saddam regime, Iraq turned into a quasi democracy and its first multi party elections were held in 2005. A number of political parties formed in the run up, split fiercely along ethnic lines[1]. The results showed just about 10% support for secularist parties. Kurds and Arab

---

dalits/25651-4.html?from=prestory

1 Can Three Become One? A look at the divided factions of the Middle East, William Beaman, Mar 2006, Reader's Digest, http://www.rd.com/can-three-become-one/article21772.html

Sunnis each form about 20% of the population and their respective parties received about similar share of the vote. Shias form the majority with about 55–60% of the population and they captured the largest chunk of votes at 47%. Since 2005 Iraq has been caught in sectarian violence and instability. This involved almost daily bomb attacks in crowded areas like marketplaces and mosques and death squad killings using torture. Amidst this factional violence many Iraqis longed for the pre-invasion days when they could count on law and order as well as basic amenities like electricity and water. Some of the national level leaders like Allawi remained secular but problem of sectarianism and division was greatest at the grassroots where petty hoodlums sought power through divisive means and imposed their own orthodox views through vigilantism.

The national oil wealth was also at the heart of this conflict.[1] The northern Kurdish and the southern Shia regions are where the oil wealth is concentrated. Both the communities wanted a federal structure with autonomy over administration and resources. This would have ensured most of the wealth was kept within their respective regions and did not have to be shared with others. The middle Arab Sunni region wanted a stronger central government else they stood to be excluded from the precious resource. Since 2009, situation stabilized somewhat as the national level leaders sought more unity and Iraqi security forces took greater charge. Violence came down but politics remained split along a multitude of factions. In the 2010 elections, an overwhelming 86 political groups vied for power.[2] Most of these were local opportunists who had cultivated small vote blocs split along sectarian and ethnic lines. As a result, post the March 2010 elections, a government was yet to be formed even 5 months down the line as the votes were fragmented among myriads of groups.[3]

Divisive calls, while on the surface seem like identity wars, underneath they are usually attempts at cornering the national resources. In India, caste divisions are to corner job reservations, in Iraq, the oil wealth. Likewise,

---

1   Resolving Shia, Sunni and Kurdish Claims over Oil Revenue in Iraq, Alvin Rabushka, Hoover Institution, Stanford University, http://www.hoover.org/research/projects-and-programs/russian-economy/6024
2   Iraq's Election Results will Confirm, but not Bestow Power, Ben Tanosborn, 8 Mar 2010, Middle east Online, http://www.middle-east-online.com/english/?id=37700
3   Iraq's Long Road to a Government, Analysis of the 2010 Iraqi Parliamentary elections, Marina Ottaway and Danial Kaysi, 26 May 2010, Carnegie Endowment for International Peace, http://www.carnegieendowment.org/publications/index.cfm?fa=view&id=40852

in Nigeria too, post independence, political parties tried to redraw the regional lines such that the Igbo tribe was kept out of sharing the national oil wealth, which led to a civil war. A contrast to these divided fighting nations is Libya, which has never attempted democracy. Its two distinct regions, Tripolitania and Cyrenaica have often been under different rules in the past but were united along with Fezzan in 1951 as Libya became an independent nation. The oil wealth is concentrated in the Tripolitania and Fezzan regions.[1] But no ethnic or regional divides have occurred in the nation and there are no conflicts involving sharing of wealth between regions. Libya is ruled as one nation and over time, the historical regions have given way to a number of districts.

In a democracy, on the other hand, parties differentiate themselves by aligning with specific sections and build loyalty through inciting hatred against each other. This is leading to divided societies where existing divisions are turning into deep fissures at the hands of election winning process in a democracy. To save it from itself, democracy should not be allowed to proliferate in such a chaotic manner. There should be restrictions on parties' formation, campaigning and results reporting along such divisive lines that stand to threaten a nation's long term unity and stability.

The Anti-Something Campaign

This is a variation of the divisive game where a political leader uses a specific hate target or a decoy on which all the problems are blamed. This decoy could be a minority within the country, a neighboring nation or a world power. Looking at earlier part of the century, one democracy example cannot be ignored, that of Adolf Hitler. He was a charismatic speaker and his fascist, hate-based nationalist, anti Semitic and anti communist agenda packaged nicely as "Good for Germany" appealed widely to the lower and middle classes. Even his election plank of giving Jews' jobs to deserving Germans struck a chord with a large number of unemployed Germans at that time. The Nazis thus rose to power in the 1930s using a campaign blaming all of Germany's economic problems on the Jews. In reality, Germany was suffering from heavy reparations post World War I as well as the worldwide depression. But Hitler successfully managed to make the electorate focus their miseries on the minority community. The strategy paid off and

---

1 Libyan Oil Industry, Country Studies, http://www.country-studies.com/libya/industry.html

in the July 1932 elections, the Nazi Party won 230 seats, making it the largest party[1] in the parliament (although it fell short of a majority in the 608-seat parliament). It also won the subsequent November 1932 elections. In 1933, Hitler was appointed Chancellor. In his own words, "How fortunate for governments that the people they administer don't think." After coming to power, he modified the constitution and assumed absolute powers, not unlike what happens in many democracies in the developing world. It led to a tragic turn for the minority community as well as a world war which was to claim an unprecedented over 50 million lives.

In modern times, political parties and leaders use this "anti-something" strategy with abandon. "Anti-rich" is standard rhetoric in most developing world democracies, where the real problem is the small size of the economy, but the populace can easily be made to believe all their problems are due to the rich who are exploiting them. As communist Russia and China realized, eliminating this small class does not solve the problems. However, in most democracies it is a powerful factor to play on and has been used with considerable success. "Anti-West" is a popular decoy in all of the Middle Eastern nations although their real focus should be on how to capitalize on their oil wealth in modernizing their economies. They have not widened their industrial base and oil price fluctuations determine their entire fortunes. In Zimbabwe, Robert Mugabe's government mismanaged the economy but the decline was blamed on the white farmers. Not only did that deflect attention from other problems that could have been solved, it brought on the wrath of international community and resulted in sanctions that have further ruined its economy. It appears that in times of economic turmoil, most political leaders find it easier to create elaborate decoys, usually a minority community or another nation to externalize the blame on, than to promote a coherent strategy to take their nations forward. That allows them to escape responsibility for fixing these problems through a positive plan of action. The hatred and violence unleashed thereafter comes back and destroys these nations too in the end. It is a "lose all" strategy which no one finally benefits from it.

---

1 "How Hitler Became a Dictator," Jacob G Hornberger, 28 Jun 2004, *Freedom Daily*, http://www.fff.org/freedom/fd0403a.asp

Other Lesser Evils

There are many other election winning strategies and tactics that need mentioning. But it is important to note that all of the following are perhaps better classified as imperfections of the system. Any other system, when analyzed in depth would also throw up equal or more fallacies. They are being called lesser evils because they are not fatal flaws of democracy which the already discussed strategies of rule by division, religious manipulation and voter bribing are.

DEMOCRATIC DYNASTIES—BY CHOICE

One of the central ideas of the Age of Enlightenment was opposition to inherited privilege, a concept key to establishing a fair society with equal opportunities. The idea was shaped by commercial factors as much as philosophical thought. On account of expanding trade with Asia and the Americas, a new class arose into prominence, that of merchants. Their growing power was accompanied by a sense of pride in their earnings as a result of individual merit and hard work unlike the inherited wealth of landed aristocracy. Whereas individualism had been emphasized even during the Renaissance, it now became a core societal value. Respect for achievement over inherited privilege was one of the key progressive elements of this era that set Europe apart from rest of the world. Democracy that followed much later naturally adopted these principles.

However, a similar social revolution has not yet taken place in most of the developing nations. While modern education and opening up has brought some changes, respect for familial and inherited social status remains an over-riding value in the majority. This manifests itself in a myriad ways including the way people make their democratic choices. During their struggles for independence from colonial rule or autocracies, the freedom fighters became important national leaders. People have subsequently turned the descendants of these leaders into the new ruling dynasties. Political party leadership thus passes hands in the form of inheritance to the offspring or other family members of the leader. Even though several of these political protégés have made good leaders, essentially this does undermine the core idea of a democracy which should ensure a government by merit as adjudged by people and not inherited rule.

In many developing countries, inherited party leadership is a foregone conclusion, even solemnized in a passing leader's will. In Pakistan, Zulfikar Bhutto founded the Pakistan People's Party (PPP) in 1967. Post his execution, his daughter, Benazir Bhutto, announced in 1978 that she was assuming party leadership as per her father's will[1], though technically her mother assumed the chairmanship. Keeping up with the tradition, post Benazir's assassination in 2007, the party leadership devolved to her son Bilawal as per Benazir's will[2]. Since he was only 19 years old, he was named as the titular head till he completes his education. In the meantime, Bhutto's widower Asif Ali Zardari continues running the party. This is reminiscent of the age-old aristocratic times—only then the succession feuds used to be bloodier and now the party leadership is passed on as a matter of will. Likewise in Bangladesh, both the dominant national parties endorse dynastic legacies. The Awami league leader Sheikh Hasina is the daughter of Sheikh Mujibur Rahman, the first premier of Bangladesh, and BNP leader Khalida Zia, the widow of General Ziaur Rahman—the first leader of that party.[3] Sri Lanka, Indonesia, the Philippines, and others have similar legacies.[4]

Likewise in India, the family of the first Prime Minister, Jawaharlal Nehru, continues to hold the dynastic reins even sixty years after independence. Here the situation is unique where the supposed dynasty wants to give up its hold on power but continually is pressured back into it by the party due to their ability to garner votes. Indira Gandhi's son, Rajiv Gandhi, reluctantly joined politics. Post his assassination, his widow, Sonia Gandhi stayed out of politics. The Congress party started disintegrating and Sonia finally buckled under immense pressure, some of it manipulative, to assume party leadership in 1998. Subsequently her son Rahul Gandhi, the heir apparent, also joined politics after a lot of hesitations and has talked about holding primaries to determine party leadership instead of his assumed leadership. He has traveled extensively to remote parts of India and spoken

---

1 Pakistan People's Party – Past and Present, A chronology, Fakhar Zaman, 2001, http://ppp.org.au/Downloads/chronology.pdf

2 Benazir Bhutto's Will Names Son as Successor, says Newsweek, Robert Fenner, 29 Dec 2007, Bloomberg, http://www.bloomberg.com/apps/news?pid=newsarchiv e&sid=axeFVmdH7stw&refer=home

3 Some Thoughts on Dynastic and Military Rule in Bangladesh, Faheem Haider, 17 Feb 2010, Foreign Policy Blogs Network, FPB, http://bangladesh.foreignpolicyblogs. com/2010/02/17/some-thoughts-on-dynastic-and-military-rule-in-bangladesh/

4 Politics of Dynasty Knows no Boundaries, 15 Dec 2001, Culture Briefings, Geo-travel Research Center, http://www.culturebriefings.com/articles/poldynty.html

strongly against the prevailing oppression of *Dalits* in India. So perhaps not all dynasties are power mongers but may be pulled into it through people's free choice, in essence through democracy.

Part of the supposed dynastic protégés' reluctance is that politics in the developing world is not always a lucrative job. Subservient to divisive factors and violence at the grassroots, the national leaders have found it difficult to bring in change for a more progressive rule. Also, most of these families have suffered enormous personal losses as many of the leaders were assassinated. Benazir Bhutto had once remarked that her few years spent studying at Harvard were the happiest years of her life. While many political progenies have been cautious in entering politics, it is the people who want these dynasties to run and identify parties with personalities rather than agendas. When a leadership post falls vacant, as in the case of death of a leader, often the party starts to disintegrate and then makes desperate attempts to rope in the surviving members of the family to keep afloat. In some places, such as India, that has even been crucial to maintaining stability.

CHOICE OF LEADERS—THE X FACTOR

In our world of audiovisual communication in the form of TV, the Internet, etc. looks, style and public-speaking skills have come to assume huge importance in the voters' minds. It is often said that nowadays, the public expects a good looking leader even though there is no proven correlation between a person's looks and his or her leadership qualities. An oft quoted example is that of Abraham Lincoln, considered neither good looking nor having a good voice. It is doubted if he could make the cut today with a style obsessed electorate. Increasingly, in elections in the UK and the US, voters pay attention not just to a candidate's style quotient but also that of his spouse.

This trend most markedly started with the first televised American presidential election debate between Kennedy and Nixon in 1960. The image and style of the two candidates became a salient feature of election analysis recorded in great detail in the annals of politics[1]. In the first debate, it was noted that Nixon didn't wear make-up, was recovering from flu and had lost weight. He also wore a gray suit, which provided little contrast

1 The Presidential Look, Bill Walsh, Billerica Minuteman, 28 Feb 2008, http://www.wickedlocal.com/billerica/news/lifestyle/columnists/x565325713

with the background set. Kennedy, on the other hand, wore a dark suit, used make-up (though he already looked tanned), and was coached on how to sit, with legs crossed, and what to do when he wasn't speaking, namely to look at Nixon. Nixon made the mistake of using dark-toned "lazy shave" face powder, and poor lighting threw deep shadows around his eyes. It is believed that the moment the two faces appeared on the screen, the entire election seemed to swing in Kennedy's direction. Nixon did learn from his mistakes and in subsequent debates, which were not watched by as wide an audience, adopted a more telegenic image. A study showed that those who had listened to the first debate on radio thought Nixon had done better but the ones who saw it on TV thought Kennedy was better. Historian Theodore White commented on the televised era, saying that "American politics has never been the same since."

According to a Princeton University study, a split-second glance at two candidates' faces is often enough to determine which one will win an election.[1] Psychologist Todorov has demonstrated that quick facial judgments can accurately predict real-world election results. His lab tests show that a rapid appraisal of the relative competence of two candidates' faces was sufficient to predict the winner in about 70 percent of the races for U.S. senator and state governor in the 2006 elections. During the presidential primaries Hillary Clinton's team once raised the question whether people use the same criteria in choosing a president as they do on the American Idol show. Going by the increasing focus on style, personal appeal, likeability at a glance, etc. this may indeed be true. More important criteria like experience, courage to make tough decisions, etc. might be taking a back seat as people surge on to elect friendly and pretty leaders. It is important to recognize this weakness in the voters' mental makeup where style predominates over substance.

SMEAR CAMPAIGNS, RUMORS, HORSE TRADING, ET AL.

Scandals are the life blood of a democracy and no election is truly complete without them. Not only they can rout a candidate in elections, they have the power to make regimes fall more than even their gross wrongdoings could. A politician's life is intertwined with potential for scandals.

---

1 To Determine Election Outcomes, Study Says Snap Judgments are Sufficient, Chad Boutin, 22 Oct 2007, News at Princeton, Princeton University, http://www.princeton.edu/main/news/archive/S19/28/30C37/index.xml?section=topstories

John Edwards, Bill Clinton, John Major, etc. all have had a taste of this bitter pill. Opposition parties as well as media keep up their efforts at dirt digging, which is not even time restricted as it can include even candidates' youthful misadventures. Nixon's Watergate, Bill Clinton's affair scandal and Cash for Peerage in the UK are some of the more notorious scandals but the democratic election landscape is mined with a multitude of small to mini to pseudo scandals.

Many of the allegations remain unproven but damage is done through the power of rumors in a democracy. Geraldine Ferraro, the first woman US vice presidential candidate in 1984, faced allegations regarding her husband's business throughout her campaign.[1] Even her father's gambling was revealed, although she was only eight years old when he died. Al Gore was trapped in a pseudo scandal[2] in 1996 when, after the cancellation of a fund raising event, he attended a luncheon at a Buddhist temple.

Opposition voices manipulated reporting on that event to make it appear like a campaign financing irregularity. Likewise many mini-scandals were created around him, though four years later these were dismissed as no evidence had been found. But scandals and rumors had done their job of discrediting him during the election.

In 2007, Shinzo Abe of Japan resigned after a year of funding scandals caused by his cabinet ministers. Four of his cabinet members resigned and one killed himself over this. The Bofors gun scandal in India started in the 1980s and refused to die down for almost two decades. It has been estimated that a higher amount has been spent in its investigations than the original amount of bribes allegedly taken by Congress Party members. In the meantime, the guns were effectively put to use in the Kargil war with Pakistan, thus also disproving that they were sub standard.[3] However, the scandal itself had a serious impact on the party. In the UK elections in 2010, Robinson, who had held Belfast East since 1979, lost over a scandal and revelations about his wife's affair. It is dispiriting to note how insubstantial an allegation or rumor can be, and still wreck political campaigns; and to see how

---

1 "Great American Presidential Election Scandals," Mike Dash, Nov 2004, *The Independent*, http://www.mikedash.com/extras/extras-intro/election

2 "Will Pseudo-Scandals Decide the Elections?" Sean Wilentz, 30 Nov 2002, *The American Prospect*, http://www.prospect.org/cs/articles?article=will_pseudoscandals_decide_the_election

3 "Why the Army Loves the Bofors Gun," 8 Jul 2009, *Press Trust of India*, NDTV, http://www.ndtv.com/news/india/why_indian_army_loves_bofors_gun.php

much national time and energy is wasted in the witch-hunt exercise. While political leaders must show rectitude in governance matters, this kind of personal mudslinging ensures that a large section of the populace avoids getting involved in politics.

The other side of this equation is the legitimate payment which is not that lucrative. In India, Member-Parliaments (MPs) are paid about $3,200 per annum[1] in nominal terms.

There are some perks like free house and free telephone calls added to this for charm. But it is no surprise then that an Indian MP's vote and support is considered perpetually for sale. There is little job security either, as at any point, by design, at least half the representatives are out of office and job. So while the risks of exposure in terms of personal security as well as privacy remain high, the legitimate rewards are hardly worth the while. Financial scandals stem from low legitimate pay as well as the nebulous area of campaign funding. Running TV campaigns requires large budgets and candidates seek contributions, often resulting in scams. In many pluralistic democracies, horse trading or buying MPs is a common occurrence too. The number of political parties can range from 20 to 200 or beyond and the national vote gets fragmented. To make up a majority, the leading parties shop for MPs through cash bribes and special positions in the government. Confidence motions on important bills too witness this kind of support-buying exercise.

All in all, scandals and smear campaigns are a perpetual strategy where parties dig up dirt on each other and the media performs an independent enthusiastic role as it looks for new stories to report. The spiraling over use of this has already led to a general disillusionment with the political class and as well has created an entry barrier for a large section of the populace who view politics as a personally dangerous territory.

VOTER IGNORANCE—LAST BUT NOT LEAST

This is not, strictly speaking, an election-winning strategy, but perhaps it is the underlying reason why most of the above-mentioned election stunts are successful.

---

1 "How Much Does an MP Earn?" George Iype, 13 Dec 2005, *Rediff News*, http://www.rediff.com/news/2005/dec/13spec.htm

A 1996 Washington Post–Harvard University survey found that more than half of Americans agreed that "Politics and government are so complicated that a person like me can't really understand what's going on." It was further estimated that roughly 36 percent of voters were "low knowledge" and only a minority of 30% were classified as "high knowledge".[1] After analyzing thousands of voter surveys, it was concluded that there was virtually no relationship between the political issues that low-knowledge voters said mattered most to them and the positions of the candidates they voted for on those issues. Political scientist Carpini noted, "It was as if their vote was random." A 1987 survey found that 45 percent of adult respondents believed that Karl Marx' communist vision "from each according to his abilities, to each according to his needs" was in the U.S. Constitution.[2] Gallup found in January 2000 that 66 percent of the public could name the host of "Who wants to be a Millionaire?" but only 6 percent knew the name of the Speaker of the House. Somin, a law professor at George Mason University, observed in a new study for the Cato Institute that voters tend to be "abysmally ignorant of even very basic political information." This may not be news to scholars, who have documented it in depressing detail for a long time.[3]

The US being the most transparent, such data exists, but all democracies suffer from voter ignorance—which even prompted the British war-time PM Winston Churchill to comment once that the best argument against democracy is a five-minute conversation with the average voter. Voters' ignorance is one of the reasons why rumors, candidates' styles or dynastic credentials, etc., work. For lack of judgment on deeper issues, voters may be falling back on emotional reasons, prejudices and the intuitive appeal of candidates to make their choices.

So these are the various rules of the game of winning elections in a democracy; this list is comprehensive but not exhaustive. While many of the issues are better classified as imperfections, some of these are fatal flaws

---

1   "The Greatest Ignorance of the Greatest Number," James Bovard, Aug 2003, *Freedom Daily*, The Future of Freedom Foundation, http://www.fff.org/freedom/fd0308d.asp

2   "Constitutional Illiteracy and Attention Deficit Democracy," James Bovard, 2006. The Future of Freedom Foundation, LewRockwell.com, http://www.lewrockwell.com/bovard/bovard28.html

3   In 1830s, Alexis de Tocqueville assessed judgment of the wise subordinated to the prejudices of the ignorant as one of the weaknesses of the US democracy. "The Tyranny of the Majority," Unlimited Power of the Majority and its Consequences — Part II, from Alexis De Tocqueville, *Democracy in America*, 1835 & 1840, Loud Mime, Free Republic, http://www.freerepublic.com/focus/news/2216858/posts

that threaten the very foundation of a democracy. Extreme reliance on direct freebies at the cost of long term investments leads to myopic governance. Use of religion to manipulate voters threatens the dimension of accountability in a democracy. The use of divisive tactics to carve out vote blocs tends to create fissured societies rather than harmonious nations. All of them stand to threaten progressive rule under a democracy. Such democracies are better classified as oxymoronic demagogies. There is a need to check the manipulative abuse of "people power" and it needs to be seen if this can be done through legislative reforms curbing the use of divisive strategies covertly or overtly.

In essence, voters do influence and shape the resultant governance in a democracy through the kind of strategies that work with them. Yet when the outcome is not liked, the blame is passed back up and the average voter is portrayed as a hapless victim. This was aptly summed up by Laurence J. Peter when he said, "Democracy is a process by which people are free to choose the man who will get the blame." The understanding of what constitutes a "free and fair" election must evolve to reflect reality. While a free election is one where parties are free to campaign and voters free from any kind of coercion, a "fair" election goes beyond that. A fair election should be a subjective analysis of what sort of issues have dominated electoral campaigns and choices. Did the electorate pay any attention to long term issues and programs or were they simply bribed and treated their votes as barter for instant benefits? Were the elections free from religious, ethnic, or caste based divisive manipulation? Unless we address the serious election-related ills that threaten democracy from within, accountability and governance will continue to erode.

CHAPTER 5. FUNDAMENTALISM: RADICAL BY CHOICE

To define it first, "Fundamentalism" is a return to orthodox dogmatic principles, usually guided by tradition or religion, and rigid adherence to them as well as their imposition on the society as a whole. Intolerance, rabble rousing, extremism and even violence are various manifestations of it. While free to choose, people have often voted for fundamentalist parties over reformist ones in the developing world. This has puzzled intellectuals who believe democracy is the instrument that would deliver these societies from their backwardness. In reality the reverse has happened. Helen Keller once said, "The heresy of one age becomes the orthodoxy of the next." Given that at any time orthodox elements are in a majority over the reformist ones, all decisions through votes would keep us grounded in the past.

Democracy in its essence is rule by the will of the majority, which need not necessarily mean progressive or benevolent rule. In most conservative developing countries, retrograde attitudes and practices abound. There are reform minded leaders as well as progressive sections in each of these societies. But they are in a minority and power, prematurely, has been placed in the hands of the conservative majority, thus making democracy a basic tool of promoting fundamentalism. Genocides, civil wars, communal riots, hate crimes, gender based oppression and rising vigilantism bear testimony to this. Let us examine the issue in depth.

South Africa: Zulu–Zuma Retrogression

In 2007, Thabo Mbeki lost his leadership of the ANC party to Jacob Zuma, who comes from the dominant Zulu tribe. Zuma evoked a brand of ethnic, gender, sexuality based identity summed up as "100% Zulu boy" in his rise to power. To begin with, Zuma's rise to leadership generated controversy as he is a polygamist who has been married five times and has over 20 children. He has been involved in several extramarital affairs and has many more children out of wedlock. Contrary to denying it, he takes great pride in it as part of the Zulu culture and has dismissed international criticism as Euro-centrism. In 2005, Zuma, 63, was charged with raping a 31-year-old woman in his house. He denied it, claiming it was consensual, and was finally acquitted. But during the trial, he used derogatory terms to refer to the accuser's body and details about her past were leaked into the press, publicly shaming her. More importantly, as the trial was in progress, huge crowds thronged outside the courthouse, chanting pro-Zuma slogans. There was even public anger at the accuser and people pelted with stones a woman mistaken for the accuser.[1] That he is a "100% Zulu boy"[2] was a term that emerged during this trial. At the time, Zuma was also the head of the National AIDS Council. During the trial he admitted not using a condom, despite knowing that the woman was HIV positive. He stated in court that he was safe as he took a shower afterwards, leading to an outcry among anti AIDS activists.

Upon his assuming ANC's leadership, the party's popularity has sky-rocketed. The society and its prevailing attitudes and practices help explain why. South Africa is dubbed the rape capital of the world, with over 500,000 rape cases every year, the majority of them involving minors, particularly babies and children below 12 years of age. This is higher than war-time atrocities in other nations. For instance Bosnia, which incurred much of the world's wrath for its rape camps, had in total 20,000 to 50,000 rapes committed through the war. South Africa has ten to twenty times that number

---

1 South African Trial Brings Rape into Public View, Carolyn Dempster, 16 Apr 2006, International Justice (ICC), Institute for War and Peace Reporting (IWPR), http://www.iwpr.net/report-news/south-african-trial-brings-rape-public-view

2 "100% Zulu Boy" : Jacob Zuma and the Use of Gender in the Run-up to South Africa's 2009 Election, Christi van der Westhuizen, 20 Apr 2009, Women's Net, http://www.womensnet.org.za/news/%E2%80%9C100-zulu-boy%E2%80%9D-jacob-zuma-and-the-use-of-gender-in-the-run-to-south-africa%E2%80%99s-2009-election

on an annual basis. It has often been said that a woman born in the country has a greater chance of being raped than learning how to read.[1] Societal shame and taboo remaining strong; most victims bear it with silence and for the cases reported, conviction rate is a mere 4%. A survey in Soweto among school children chillingly revealed that a quarter of school boys claimed gang raping was fun.[2] It was seen as a form of male bonding. Surveys show that men are brought up with a sense of entitlement where they do not believe a woman has the right to say no and rapists commonly believe they did nothing wrong. This attitude was reflected in the unanimous support for Zuma irrespective of the outcome of the trial and even anger at the woman for bringing up charges. AIDS continues to be a serious epidemic with 20% of the adult population infected with the virus but ignorance on the disease is high. Post fall of the apartheid regime, crime has risen multifold and today is the highest in the world in nations not at war.

In a society caught on such a regressive social path, people choose a leader who, to them, symbolizes their values. He further promotes a form of patriarchal male domination and regression and also links it to ethnicity. A vicious cycle takes root as a poor society inlaid with regressive norms and practices favors a leader[3] who tends to support these norms and further builds his support promoting even greater degree of retrogression. It is quintessential democracy.

Could gender related oppression, abuse of women's rights, and a high HIV incidence be curbed under such a system? Is "rule of majority" the right model for South Africa? Democracy does not seem to be working for the average populace, especially the weakest, namely women and children. What is worse is that the direction is also negative and would ensure the future is more blighted than the present. Apart from violence and crime that has already spiraled out of control, social regression will only be strengthened under democracy.

---

1 Rape — Silent War on SA Women, Carolyn Dempster, 9 Apr 2002, BBC News, http://news.bbc.co.uk/2/hi/africa/1909220.stm

2 South Africa's Rape Shock, World: Africa, 19 Jan 1999, BBC News, http://news.bbc.co.uk/2/hi/africa/258446.stm. One Quarter of South African Men Admit to Rape, Chris Dade, 22 Jun 2009, Digital Journal, http://www.digitaljournal.com/article/274547

3 Jacob Zuma : the Wrong Man for the Job, David Blair, 24 Apr 2009, Telegraph. co.uk, http://www.telegraph.co.uk/news/worldnews/africaandindianocean/southafrica/5215533/Jacob-Zuma-the-wrong-man-for-the-job.html

Rwanda—War Over, Lesson not Learnt

Africa's infamous "tribalism" provides another example. A small country in Eastern Central Africa, Rwanda shot to international fame on account of its 1994 genocide when about 800,000 people were killed and more than 250,000 women raped in a span of 100 days. Most of the atrocities were committed by the majority Hutus on the minority Tutsis. Why and how did the Hutu–Tutsi clashes come about, were they always at war?

Going back in history, the Hutus were well established in the region when the Tutsis came from the North and conquered the area about the 15th century. The Tutsi kings, or *mwamis*, thereafter continued ruling the area.[1] In modern democratic terms, this has been described as a rule of minority over majority but in the kingdoms era this was common throughout the world. India, for instance, was ruled for centuries by the Mughal Empire, which we could call the rule of a Muslim minority over a Hindu majority. These are essentially post democratic terms. Back then, the conquering empires usually ruled whatever area they conquered irrespective of majority or minority.

A small landlocked nation, roughly one tenth the size of neighboring Uganda and one hundredth of DR Congo, Rwanda also lacks any natural resources. It was not a significant or important territory to the colonial powers, like the Belgians, who continued previous policies of supporting education by missionaries and of ruling through the existing power structure. The two ethnic groups are similar in their traditions, religion and language but societal divisions remained strong and intermarriages uncommon. No doubt, the power imbalance between Tutsis and Hutus needed challenging but let us see how this was done through democracy.

In the late 1950s in the run up to independence, parties as well as the freedom movement split along ethnic lines. 1959 saw the first ever mob violence against Tutsis and several refugees fled to the neighboring countries triggering ethnic clashes in Burundi as well. Ethnic violence continued through the first decade of democracy till 1973 when Habyarimana toppled the government in a coup and suspended the constitution and the parliament. He stayed in power for almost two decades and Rwanda saw relative peace in this period. In the 1990s talks about a return to democracy were underway when Habyarimana was assassinated, sparking a civil war. In a span of 100 days 20% population of the nation was brutally wiped out and

---

1 History of Rwanda, Microsoft® Encarta® Online Encyclopedia 2009

women became a prime target for assaults. While instigated and abetted by local Hutu political groups, the mass killings and rapes were carried out by hordes of common people who simply turned upon their neighbors.[1] The large scale massacre led to an outpouring of refugees and further deaths on account of diseases and starvation. The guerilla groups created in the bordering regions played a crucial role in the even more chilling civil war that was to follow in Congo.

However in 3 months time this civil war was tamed. The Rwanda patriotic front (RPF), the military rebel wing supported by Uganda, defeated the Rwandan army and took control. A moderate Hutu assumed presidency and stabilized the nation. In 2000, Paul Kagame, the earlier RPF leader and a Tutsi, who was considered the real power behind the throne, assumed the formal presidency. Under this new single party rule, the power structure was redrawn to include both Hutus and Tutsis in the cabinet. Discrimination based on ethnicity, race or religion was prohibited and political activity centered round Hutu or Tutsi identity was outlawed. This bears a striking resemblance to Kenya under Jomo Kenyatta and KANU-party rule when that nation knew better days. Most importantly, in a continent where patriarchal values dominate, in Rwanda, women were given encouragement to study and work. It became the first African nation where women were granted a huge representation in the parliament. One third of all cabinet positions including key posts of foreign minister, education minister and importantly Supreme Court chief were accorded to women.[2] Ethnic tensions were also pacified and the government turned its attention to rebuilding the war ravaged economy. About 15 years down the line, Rwanda is on a progressive path, even being hailed as a role model[3] for others. Under a strong centralized rule, Rwanda has begun to heal and stabilize. Tutsis and Hutus coexisted peacefully for centuries and have again come to some terms in the unified strong rule. However, even after sustained initiatives, 76.6%

---

1 Rwanda: End of Tribalism, a 'Never Again' Solution, John Kimanuka, 4 May 2005, All Africa.com, http://allafrica.com/stories/200505040044.html. Echoes of Violence: Genocide in Rwanda, Darryl Li, Journal of Genocide Research, Mar 2004, The International Development Research Center (IDRC), http://www.idrc.ca/rwandagenocide/ev-108188-201-1-DO_TOPIC.html

2 Women Run the Show in a Recovering Rwanda, Stephanie McCrummen, Washington Post Foreign Service, 27 Oct 2008, http://www.washingtonpost.com/wp-dyn/content/article/2008/10/26/AR2008102602197.html

3 "Rwanda is Africa's Biggest Success Story" — Fareed Zakaria, 5 Aug 2009, *The Independent*, http://www.independent.co.ug/index.php/news/regional-news/78-regional-news/1419-rwanda-is-africas-biggest-success-story-fareed-zakaria

of Rwanda's population is below the poverty line and it still has a low per capita income. It has a long way to go.

And in any event, all is not well that ends well. Now we come to the trap of circular reasoning. To gain international support and legitimacy, Rwanda remained under pressure to whitewash its reputation through the process of elections and democracy. It held elections in 2010 and it is just as well that Paul Kagame mitigated serious opposition and staged elections to declare himself the winner. While this has earned him the criticism of Commonwealth observers, he has saved Rwanda from a fresh return to ethnically inspired politics and violence. Whatever is the need to bring in or even stage a democracy to gain legitimacy? Is delivering good governance not enough? Isn't a good government, doing all the right things, not a legitimate government in its own right? Why at all would democracy be a way "forward" for Rwanda? If Rwanda has managed to end the war, resolve its ethnic issues and work towards women's emancipation, it was not a mere coincidence. It happened as a result of committed leadership under an "empowered format." Rwanda should be a role model for nations like South Africa and even more so DR Congo, not the other way round. A turn to democracy in the 1960s is exactly what started ethnic violence in Rwanda. If implemented in earnestness, democracy would take Rwanda back in time. Then we can look away, decrying, once again, how "these people" will never understand democracy. It is the international pressure groups and opinion leaders that do not understand democracy in a developing world context. As said already, in largely destitute nations, the naïve majority easily falls prey to political opportunists who exploit the naturally existing divisions in a society to fuel fundamentalism and violence.

Based on evidence thus far, Rwanda's example seems to suggest that the mere presence of ethnic differences or tribes does not create tribal fundamentalism. Even a government dominated by a minority tribe does not; but a premature political opening up does. This was first verbalized by Kenyan President Daniel arap Moi in the 1990s when he attributed Kenyan violence to multi party democracy, not tribalism. All societies have some form of residual differences which seem to get exploited by political opportunists in most poor democracies. This gives wings to the wrong elements that play on tribal insecurities and create an environment of intolerance and violence. In the centralized, non democratic rule in the last 15 years in Rwanda, "tribalism" and its associated violence has all but disappeared (indeed, it had not existed for centuries earlier, either). It really started with the turn to the formation of political parties in the run up to independence elections in 1959.

Gross violence in Africa post 1960s has generally been attributed to the theory of tribalism. But if we look closer we find that most of these wars took place post political opening up or a turn to democracy. Tribal or sectarian warfare is not genetic to Africa, it is genetic to premature democracy in Africa, or indeed in most of the developing world, as we shall see in further examples.

RELIGIOUS FUNDAMENTALISM

Several factors have led to the rise of this banal problem of our times. Perhaps a suddenly global world necessitating interaction between mutually incomprehensible cultures is also one among the many causal factors. Further a conflict between conservatives and liberals exists in almost every society, while the issues on which they spar vary over time and nationalities.

However, being religious or conservative is not synonymous with being a fundamentalist. The latter necessarily involves preference for and proclivity towards intolerance and violence. For instance some of the old empires like the Ottomans or even some of the earlier Mughals were conservative but not fundamentalist. In fact tolerance, intermingling and communal harmony was largely encouraged to maintain stability and order within their vast territories. The fierce rise of communal hatred and intolerance seems to have reached an alarming level since the last century. As in other forms of fundamentalism discussed so far, democracy seems to have played an incendiary role. In many a democracy, religion has become a key factor in determining electoral outcomes and has got deeply intertwined with the political power game. Establishing political parties along political and economic ideologies and communicating them to the voters is a hard task in the developing world. Instead, rabble rousing to create a conservative majority in the largely poor, rural population has become a quick and easy road to political power, giving political parties and leaders instant success. Perhaps people also feel obligated by their faith to vote for a religious leaning party, fearing they are opposing their faith if they don't vote for them. Some religious bodies themselves form political parties and even want to gain direct political power. It also seems the more radical the groups, the higher their appeal to the elementary electorate. While it is true that all conservatives are not fundamentalist, in the case of political parties, this line becomes thinner over time as more radical strategies seem to work better with the electorate. Quite often the party leadership remains moderate but radical elements take over at the grassroots. As extremism rises through such a process, its impact is singularly negative on all.

Violence and intolerance propagated against others, initially, soon also turns inwards. For instance Hitler-sponsored Nazism, the most extremist example of fundamentalism in the last century, led to a disaster like none other, for everybody. Hitler too rose to power through democracy but the intolerance and extremism that he initially propagated against others soon also turned inwards. Once in power, the rule became intolerant and despotic internally as well. While millions in the world suffered on account of the war it helped bring about, it did not spare the nation that initiated it, either. Within Europe, Germany suffered the worst war casualties, an estimated over 6–8 million deaths. Even in the present times, most nations which have been taken over by extremist elements have no doubt caused tremendous harm to others but also subsequently suffered violence and despotism internally as well. Let us look at examples of some of the democratic and non democratic regimes to understand its link with fundamentalism a little better.

Egypt—Steadfast Secularism

A group of army officers led by General Nasser took control of the nation in 1952. Initially, Egypt took the lead in opposition to Israel and helped create the PLO. But by the mid 1970s, Egypt's economy started to feel the strains of costly wars with Israel as well as the nationalization of industries that it had undertaken. In the meantime, Anwar Sadat became the leader and signed a comprehensive peace accord with Israel in 1979 and also started gearing the country towards a market economy. However, there was little public support for his peace initiatives, and in 1981 he was assassinated by a radical. Hosni Mubarak assumed the presidency and promised some opening up but was staunchly against religious parties and hence curbed their political freedom. Here, it ought to be understood that Egypt remained a conservative society, and religion continues to play an important role in people's lives. The Muslim Brotherhood has been a vital organization that endorses charitable initiatives like the distribution of food and medicine to the poor, not unlike such activities under other religions as well. The Brotherhood continues operating unhindered in all such initiatives. But Egypt's secularist regime opposed its political involvement[1] and generally any religious party involvement in politics.

With a vast arid desert and limited natural resources, Egypt developed its tourism industry by preserving its heritage sites well and developing a world class infrastructure around them. The tourism sector became an important foreign exchange earner and contributed significantly to employment generation in the country[2]. Egypt's moderate, tolerant policies helped foster an industry friendly environment and investment in education has allowed Egypt to make a foray into the IT industry as well. In the 1990s Egypt faced terrorism within its borders when radical groups murdered secular minded politicians and writers and attacked tourist destinations. They tried to overthrow the government and made a failed assassination attempt on Mubarak. The peace treaty with Israel remained widely unpopular but the military regime remained steadfast in its commitment to it and even sponsored meetings to promote peace between Israel and Palestine. While resisting extremism internally or from externally sponsored elements, Egypt has retained its character. It has a distinct culture and a vibrant atmosphere evident in Cairo—a city of a thousand minarets. People are free to enjoy and seek comfort in the spiritual aspects of their religion. Yet the peace and harmony allows them to also enjoy a good economic life as well as reasonable law and order.

In the 2000s, Mubarak allowed some political opening up but continued suppressing religious parties. Instigated by some of these groups, people have often demanded more orthodox norms and laws but Egypt continued to maintain its moderate environment. International pressure for democracy remains high but thus far Mubarak has held onto centralized rule. Egypt seems to be doing well for its citizens; a turn to democracy would likely destabilize it and Egypt would do well to stay away from democracy and continue enjoying its tolerant and peaceful culture.

---

1 The Draft Party Platform of Egyptian Muslim Brotherhood — Foray into politics, Nathan J Brown, Amr Hamzawy, Carnegie Paper Jan 2008, Carnegie Endowment for International Peace, http://www.carnegieendowment.org/publications/index. cfm?fa=view&id=19835

2 Tourism Contributes to Growth of Egypt's Economy, Abdel Latif Wahba and Alaa Shahine, 11 Feb 2010, eTN, http://www.eturbonews.com/14374/ tourism-contributes-growth-egypts-economy

Now let us turn our attention to some of the democracies.

Iraq, Afghanistan, Pakistan

In many of the nations that have turned to democracy in the last decade, the results do not seem too favorable. Violence and anarchy seem to be on a general rise and laws seem more regressive particularly for women than they were under some of the previous unitary regimes. This seems to go in line with the ideology espoused by radical elements that control the poor, rural and orthodox majority at the grassroots. Most of these radical groups seem to have little to contribute in terms of economic development agendas but use rabble rousing to build vote blocs and gain easy access to power and riches. American columnist Ben Tanosborn summed this up nicely in his observation of the Iraq elections, "And just as often, many of the characters involved in those elections turned out to be the same old autocratic rulers now dressed in democratic vestments, their faces painted as if white mimes. The same old cast of characters—good old commissars, tribal leaders, and other power-laden chieftains, their names appearing in the ballot box after a democratic whitewashing of sorts had been done to accommodate the apostles of the new political religion, said to be democracy."[1]

Likewise, in Pakistan, post return to democracy in 2008, in many provinces like Punjab, several of the earlier banned militant groups have now become elected representatives.[2] Sipah-e-Sahaba, a militant group was solicited by Nawaz Sharif as well as the Pakistan People's party during the elections. So in essence, the militant and radical elements have acquired democratic power at the grassroots and national parties have to woo them to gain the arithmetic support to form a majority. The resultant governance thereby tends towards radicalism.

While analyzing some of the non democratic conservative regimes in the region, like Saudi Arabia, Fareed Zakaria[3] points out that many of these Arab rulers are autocratic, corrupt and heavy handed. But they are still more liberal, tolerant and pluralistic than what would replace them if they were

---

1 Iraq's election results will confirm but not bestow power, Ben Tanosborn, Middle East Online, 2010, http://www.middle-east-online.com/english/?id=37700
2 Pakistan Attacks Point to Resurgent Extremism, Saeed Shah, 6 Apr 2010, Global Post, http://www.globalpost.com/dispatch/pakistan/100406/pakistan-suicide-bombings-funerals-consulate?page=0,1
3 The Future of Freedom, Fareed Zakaria, Chapter 4, The Islamic Exception, (W.W. Norton & Company, Inc. 2003)

to turn democratic. This observation also seems to hold true for rulers from the military in the region. In Egypt, Pakistan, and Bangladesh as well as Algeria, military rulers have tended towards secularism and modernization whereas the democracies towards fundamentalism.

To sum up, as seen in these different manifestations of fundamentalism, be it tribal, social or religious, a sudden political opening up in the developing world has often led to genocides, militancy, gender based oppression and a general rise in intolerance and violence in many nations. A key reason is that the majority in most of these societies is rural, poor and conservative. It remains hard for parties to credibly communicate differentiation along political and economic policies. It is also harder to implement long term programs that bear fruits slowly. Inciting and exciting this populace along divisive, regressive or fundamentalist lines becomes an easy way for political opportunists to gain political power. In most of the developing-world societies, there is a section of the progressive educated urban class that could be classified as "discerning voters"—they are harder to incite to violence and intolerance but they are still an electoral minority. It is important to assess the state of the *demos* who form a majority to determine what quality and character the resultant *demo*cracies will have.

"Democratization and modernization" are almost used as synonymous terms in our world, especially as democracy is propagated as the right solution for everybody. But in the Western context, the societies first underwent modernization for centuries through the Scientific Revolution, the Enlightenment Age and several revolutionary initiatives alongside industrial development. As these nations became modernized and developed, they gradually brought in democracy and the resultant outcome was democracy and modernity. So, in their context, modernization preceded democratization, not the other way round. Bringing democracy into an elementary society does not seem to bring in modernization. To the contrary many of the age old regressive norms and practices are reinforced rather than challenged. A premature "rule of majority" becomes a means of sanctifying regressive attitudes and practices in an elementary society. Like Rwanda, many of these nations have seen reformist leaders under other models but a turn to democracy unequivocally has led them towards fundamentalism.

CHAPTER 6. SECESSION — THE RIGHT TO SELF DETERMINATION OR NATIONAL DISINTEGRATION?

In the old times when kings and emperors ruled the world, wars were essentially expansionist in nature where a ruler sought to increase his domain and power. Democracy's wars are essentially secessionist in nature, when people seek not to control larger resource bases but to splinter and make their own tiny little nations where they can live with just their kind. This is also encouraged internationally under "the right to self determination." In reality it has been noticed that separatism accepted for one region tends to set off a chain reaction in a nation, with several other regions demanding similar independence. Usually there are strong political motives behind such movements as the provincial politicians seek to be bigger fishes in smaller ponds. In the old times of empires such states would not have had any stability as they would be indefensible and would soon be run over by neighboring larger kingdoms. In the new world order, however, they are offered international legitimacy and protection. But in each newly splintered state, a new minority is created who now feels threatened and insecure and demands a similar secession; and so on and so forth.

Countless nations like Yugoslavia have been torn apart by this misguided process in the name of the right to self determination, through endless referenda asking regions if they want to stay together or to separate. There are hardly any instances where people have come responded that they wanted to stay together in a country rather than forming a small little country of their own with just their kind. After long periods of intermingling, when nations are divided, people often engage in an unprecedented communal bloodbath leading to loss of life as well as an outpouring of refugees. This happened during the partition of India and Pakistan, during the splintering of Yugoslavia, in the three decade long civil war in Sri Lanka and countless other movements. A change in our basic assumptions is called for to encourage people to intermingle and find common ground rather than always look for differences and demand secession.

YUGOSLAVIA—DEMOCRATIC DISINTEGRATION

Yugoslavia, the land of southern Slavs, was a nation created at the end of World War I. Prior to that, most of it was part of the Austro–Hungarian Empire when only Serbia & Montenegro was an independent state. Post collapse of the Empire during World War I, Italy occupied Croatia and Slovenia. Threatened by this development, the Croats and Slovenes immediately sought to secede and merge with Serbia on grounds of ethnic homogeneity with the latter. In 1918 the kingdom of Serbs, Croats and Slovenes was founded under King Aleksander of Serbia. In the subsequent move to form a republican government, political parties split along regional lines and started bickering over power and resource sharing issues. While newly formed, already nationalist separatist movements started in the varied provinces, most aggressively among Croats. In order to curb this factionalism, King Aleksander[1] suspended the constitution as well as the parliament and banned political party formation along regional or religious lines. He further redrew the regional boundaries to create new *banovines* or provinces designed to break up historical identities. In 1934 he was assassinated by separatists but the new Regent Prince continued his pan-Yugoslavian policies. During World War II, the Croats allied with Germany and Italy to gain independence. Under Axis occupation, the Croatian puppet regime undertook Yugoslavia's first ethnic cleansing as thousands were murdered. On the other hand, the communists struggled against the Axis powers and post World War II won control over the nation under Josep Broz Tito.

While a Croat by origin, Tito had a pan-Yugoslavian following which proved crucial for stabilizing the factional republic. A federal structure was

---

1 King Alexander I, FirstWorldWar.com, http://www.firstworldwar.com/bio/alexander_serbia.htm

created with six republics—Serbia, Croatia, Bosnia & Herzegovina, Slovenia, Macedonia and Montenegro, and two autonomous provinces within Serbia: Kosovo and Vojvodina. Yugoslavia slowly distanced itself from the USSR and was considered one of the most open and progressive of all communist states at the time. The federal structure as well as Tito's credibility in all the republics helped stabilize the union. Upon Tito's death in 1980, lacking any clear successor in leadership, the nation started to come undone. This was further precipitated by a deepening economic crisis, akin to that of most other socialist economies at the time. Ethnic tensions mounted in all regions. Slovenia and Croatia, long resentful of having to share their resources with less developed republics, sought greater autonomy and looser ties with the federation. Kosovo, with an Albanian majority, demanded the status of a republic.

At this time, the federal presidency consisted of the representatives of all 6 republics and 2 provinces as well as the JNA, the Yugoslav People's army. The heads of these republics and provinces took one-year rotation terms as head of the federal party and congress. So, while nationalist divisive tendencies soared in each of the republics, Yugoslavia as a nation was without a head as a pan-Yugoslavian leadership succession had not developed under Tito's cult rule. In 1988, Serbian leader Slobodan Milošević tried to control divisionism but his method of centralizing authority and reducing Kosovo's autonomy sent the wrong signals. The regional republican leaders used the slogan "Today Kosovo, tomorrow us" to play on people's insecurities and mistrust, which helped them further their separatist agendas. In 1990 the Congress was convened where Slovenes and Croats demanded autonomy. They were voted down, prompting them to leave the congress, which led to the formal dissolution of the federal party.

By 1990, communist regimes had fallen all across Eastern Europe and a new wave was sweeping the region, under the frothy headings of "people power," "referenda" and "democracy." Yugoslavia too held multiparty elections in its republics, and predictably, regional parties with nationalist ambitions won elections in each one. Slovenia and Croatia further held a referendum on secession and voted themselves out of Yugoslavia, declaring their independence unilaterally in 1991.[1] In six months' time this was

---

1 Timeline: The Former Yugoslavia, Borgna Brunner and David Johnson, Dates of various referenda and declaration of independence in former Yugoslav republics, Information Please® Database, © 2007 Pearson Education, Inc. http://www.infoplease.com/spot/yugotimeline1.html

recognized by the European committee. While Slovenia, always a bit of an outlier, seceded relatively peacefully, civil war started in Croatia. Over the decades, Serbs and Croats had intermingled and now the Serbs, the new minority, sought autonomy too—which ironically Croatia was not willing to give. Secession and international recognition of Croatia and Slovenia served as a catalyst for rest of the republics to seek independence as well.

Soon Bosnia and Herzegovina held a referendum and declared independence in 1991. This was the most diverse of all republics, with a significant presence of three communities: Bosniaks, Croats and Serbs. Predictably, a three-way conflict erupted where the communities turned on each other and undertook ethnic cleansing and other brutalities. Serbian and Croatian forces too got involved in supporting their respective communities. Bosniaks in the eastern bordering region suffered some of the worst brutalities at the hands of the Serbian forces. Most diverse of all, the Bosnian republic took the longest to stabilize.

In the meantime, Macedonia too declared its independence but was allowed to go more peacefully. Kosovo stepped up its agitation for independence. Serbia crushed this rebellion mercilessly and was in turn pounded by NATO forces for two months. While international support for Kosovo's Albanian majority mounted, it created 250,000 Serbian and Roma refugees, the new minority, seeking escape from reprisals. In 2008 Kosovo declared its independence.

Serbia and Montenegro had existed as an independent state before the formation of Yugoslavia in the early 20th century, but now even Montenegro decided to split. A referendum was organized in 2006 and 56% of the population voted for secession; it became an independent state. There was hardly any underlying tension in this region but it just seemed fashionable at the time to secede and be independent.

Yugoslavia's break-up resulted in civil wars, ethnic cleansing, new separatist movements and refugee crises. The successor regimes in most of the newly independent nations elected semi-authoritarian and bitterly nationalist regimes. In the ensuing democratic republics, uniformly all elections have been a setback for moderate non-nationalists; hardliners have won landslide victories. As a result of the wars, religious identification and adherence to religious rules has risen among Bosniaks, Croats, and Serbs.[1]

1　Religion and Ethnic Identity Formation in the Former Yugoslavia, Alexander Mirescu,　http://www.georgefox.edu/academics/undergrad/departments/soc-

Many Bosniak women have adopted Islamic dress styles that had not been common, at least in cities, before the war. During the communist era, Yugoslavia was considered one of the better-off states but since its dismantling, all except Slovenia lag behind other countries in Eastern Europe. Most of them today are feeble, minor states with small population bases. Slovenia, FRY Macedonia and Kosovo each have a population of about 2 million and the smallest, Montenegro, just 0.6 million.

It could be asked why a small region like Kosovo, with its Albanian majority, did not demand a merger with the adjoining Albania. Why independence? Obviously the root impetus for their action was not ethnicity but provincial ambition. Anyhow, all Yugoslavia's successor states suffer from ethnic conflicts, crime, sluggish economies and bitter regional animosity as a result of the war.

It all started with Slovenia and Croatia, the better-off regions, who did not want to share their resources with the rest and demanded secession. But going back in history, it was on the basis of ethnic differences with the Austrian (later Austro–Hungarian) Empire that they wanted to be a part of Yugoslavia and promoted the idea of a land of Southern Slavs. But now economic differences came to the fore. By that kind of logic no nation in the world can stay together, as there will either be ethnic or economic differences between provinces.

Splitting up nations to deal with diversity seems to have come at a great cost both in terms of life and of economic devastation. Further, the creation of each state has generated a new set of minorities who now feel marginalized. Thus, secession just alters the game where a minority becomes the majority and creates a new minority.

The political solution ought to have been more sophisticated than a referendum-based indiscriminate right to self determination. The biggest factor in Yugoslavia's breakup was lack of a national-level leadership or authority after Tito's demise. A headless nation is an open invitation to factional political opportunists which international forces inadvertently aided through the misguided notion of the "right to self determination." Instead, if international pressure had been applied to all the warring republics to agree on a central leadership, Yugoslavia might have remained a nation of some standing, instead of being fragmented into weaker units.

Yugoslavia is by now a case study in secession and violent disintegra-tion. It proves in no unclear terms that once secession is allowed in one or two provinces, it snowballs into a total disintegration of the country. That supports the position of other countries that take a strong stand against al-lowing one province to secede out of fear that others will follow suit.

While violent secessionist movements abound in the world,[1] there is an example of an utterly peaceful breakup that helps give a more complete pic-ture of dynamics at play.

CZECH AND SLOVAKIA—THE "VELVET DIVORCE"

Post the collapse of the Austro–Hungarian Empire in World War I, Czechoslovakia was created as an independent state. It was the first time in over 1,000 years that Czechs and Slovaks had come together as one po-litical entity. Due to proximity and a history of having been ruled under similar European empires, the two regions shared a similar heritage but still had substantial economic and religious differences. The Czechs were economically more advanced than the predominantly agrarian Slovaks and while the Czechs had rejected the authority of the religious clergy, most Slovaks were staunchly Catholic. The two split in 1939 after the German occupation but were united once again by the communists following World War II. The USSR controlled the nation and kept political expression and dissent to a minimum. In the context of major shifts in the international power structure, of which the political reforms in the USSR under Mikhail Gorbachev were emblematic, hope for political reforms and independence grew in Czechoslovakia.

In a nation used to an absence of violence, this era marked a continu-ation of its legacy and the smooth and peaceful transition was termed the "Velvet Revolution." In June 1990, free elections were held and of course the parties split along historic regional lines: Czech leader Václav Havel won in Czech lands and Slovak Vladimír Mečiar in Slovakia. While the nation had held together in harmony for most part of the 20th century, the political opening up cost it its unity. Czechs wanted a more market-oriented econo-my and unified rule whereas the Slovakian leadership was more left-leaning as far as the economy, with autonomy politically. The differences intensi-

---

1 Secession, National Sovereignty and Territorial Integrity, Sam Vaknin, World in Conflict and Transition, Buzzle.com, http://www.buzzle.com/articles/secession-national-sovereignty-and-territorial-integrity.html

fied in the 1992 parliamentary elections where regional parties won in the respective regions. Within a month Slovakia, the smaller province, declared its independence unanimously. Despite being opposed to the split, Havel accepted the decision and the two sides negotiated the dissolution of the state and a division of its assets and lands.[1]

This secession was smooth and both sides remained utterly peaceful. This was possible in part because the two peoples had never intermingled much, even during the unified communist rule. In Slovakia, Czechs were a small proportion and in the Czech Republic, Slovaks constituted just 3% of the population. Because the communities were geographically separate, no refugees were created. There are some tensions between Slovaks and the Hungarian minority in Slovakia and between Czechs and Romas in the Czech Republic, but none between Czechs and Slovaks. Even in Yugoslavia, the republics that were most homogeneous, like Slovenia, seceded peacefully whereas Bosnia, the most intermingled, suffered the most. Czechs and Slovaks since have enjoyed amicable relations and even cooperated in trade.[2] Both are now small entities within the EU and at times Czech leaders have expressed frustrations with the powerful hold of Germany.

However this velvet divorce of sorts has set a new precedent. When Belgian regional parties could not agree to a power-sharing formula, post the 2007 elections, they started contemplating a split[3] along Czechoslovakian lines, after having been in existence as one nation for nearly two centuries. Splitting up a nation along regional political lines can seem like a simple solution as compared to years of negotiations, compromise and wrangling. The presence of EU and NATO anyway provides an overall umbrella of security. But is this the future of the world under democracy?

Czechs and Slovaks have friendly relations and at the time of break up, polls showed that most of the citizens were actually against the split. Conflicting political ideologies of regionally split political parties played a central role in the break up. Allowing national parties to form out of regional skews seems to be the source of the conflict. This is also the problem in

---

1 Czechoslovakia's Velvet Divorce, Phil Barta, East/West Letter, Vol 1 No. 4, Fall 1992, http://www.okno.com/ewltr/archive/vol1/cz-divorce-vln4.pdf

2 Reflections on the Split of Czechoslovakia, Ten Years on, Martin Hrobsky, 27 Dec 2002, © 1996–2010 Český rozhlas, http://www.radio.cz/en/article/35872

3 Belgium Studies Czechoslovakia Breakup, Jan Sliva, 11 Sept 2007, The Washington Post, http://www.washingtonpost.com/wp-dyn/content/article/2007/09/11/AR2007091101144.html

Belgium that we will examine under the section on coalitions. In Czecho-slovakia, the crux of the problem was a lack of pan-national parties.

If parties are allowed to form based on regional identities, sooner or later they will come to espouse mutually exclusive goals. Does this call for more evolved mechanisms to ensure that national governments represent a na-tional character? While a federal structure can be created to accommodate regional priorities, it has to be balanced with unifying mechanisms that en-sure national parties have a pan-national presence. At this time, that seems to be lacking in most democracies. But there are exceptions, like Germany.

GERMANY—STRENGTH IN UNITY

In case of both Yugoslavia as well as Czechoslovakia, a reason often cited for the break up is that they never existed as one nation historically. But that measure could be applied to innumerable nations round the world. A contrasting case here would be Germany, which was formed in 1871. The central aspect of its history was verbalized by writers Goethe and Schiller when they lamented, "Germany? But where is it? I cannot find that country."[1] Until 1871 there was no Germany. Several of these territories that constitute Germany today were divided into a myriad kingdoms, duchies, fiefdoms, etc. Although at times part of common empires, they often waged wars with each other and represented diverse cultures. Only when Chancellor Otto von Bismarck led Prussia's victory over Austria and France, Germany was first established under Emperor Wilhelm I in 1871. Despite the nation's tur-bulent turn during the two World Wars, at the time of this writing it is seen that Germany survived as one nation. In fact, when post-communist states like Czechoslovakia and Yugoslavia were breaking up, Germany was undergoing the opposite as it reunified East and West Germany in about 1990.

The core to its strength and resilience is its unique federalism as out-lined in its constitutional framework, the Basic Law. As the German finance minister Wolfgang Schäuble clarified its central tenet—"If you want to create a federal organization, you must be ready to have a certain amount of redistribution within it. Stronger and weaker states, both have their

---

1 Germany — History, US Department of State background Note, Country profiles — Germany, Information Please® Database, © 2007 Pearson Education, Inc. http://www.infoplease.com/country/profiles/germany.html

responsibility"[1]. The Basic Law stipulates that it be possible to compare living conditions throughout Germany and so there has been a tradition of explicit transfers from richer to poorer states. Staying true to this, Germany immersed itself in the task of bringing the standard of living in East Germany up to that of its Western counterpart. The process was not easy given the lack of infrastructure in the latter as well as industrial inefficiency that it inherited from its communist past. Initially, as old structures were broken down, reunification led to chaos and violence in East Germany. That was brought under control and Germany kept investing in the laggard region. Angela Merkel, Chancellor since 2005, even hails from East Germany, though that has not been a big factor in her political ascent. There are other tenets to the basic law that ensure the national character of its national government that we will discuss under "Coalitions," but Germany has proven in practice that it is possible to stay united despite diversity.

While the merits of unity and stability cannot be emphasized enough, we still need to understand another aspect of secession. What about cases where a region considers itself an occupied land rather than an integral part of a nation? Let us look at East Timor.

INDONESIA—SAVED FROM FOLLOWING YUGOSLAVIA

Indonesia gained its independence in 1945. Initial attempts at democracy were abandoned on account of anarchy and political factionalism. Sukarno, the president, soon assumed authoritarian powers. He was outmaneuvered in the late 1960s by General Suharto, who ruled Indonesia for 30 years. During this period, the nation experienced modernization and an economic boom and Suharto enjoyed good relations with the West, bringing in foreign direct investment. Geographically a diverse archipelago, Indonesia had from time to time experienced insurgency in some of its parts; this was suppressed by the strong central regime. In the 1990s, the world order changed. Very few nations continued with overt authoritarian rule, and demands for democracy were mounting in Indonesia too. In 1997 and 1998 the Asian financial crisis triggered an economic downturn in Indonesia. This increased popular discontent, and in response to protests, Suharto resigned in 1998. Elections were held in 1999 and a coalition of two parties

---

1 Schäuble interview: Berlin's strictures, Quentin Peel, Financial Times, 19 May 2010, http://www.ft.com/cms/s/0/b82f3e3c-6377-11df-a844-00144feab49a.html

assumed leadership. Soon, much of the country was embroiled in an ethnic, religious and political upheaval. A part of this new culture of factionalism was renewed demands for secession in East Timor.

Indonesia is an archipelago of about 17,500 islands with a total population of 230 million. Of these Timor is a small island with a population of 2 million, split half and half between East and West Timor, even though the two peoples have similar religion, language and culture. During colonial rule, the Dutch colonized Indonesia including West Timor, but East Timor was occupied by the Portuguese. While West Timor was a part of independent Indonesia, Portuguese colonial rule in East Timor ended only in 1975. A leftist group, Fretilin, declared independence but Indonesia soon occupied and annexed this half of the island. East Timorese separatism or its "freedom struggle" thereafter was brutally crushed by Suharto's regime. In 1999 however, with return of democracy in Indonesia, East Timor stepped up its demands for independence. A UN sponsored referendum was held in East Timor and of course the majority voted for secession. Violent clashes started in the island by pro Indonesia militias aided and abetted by the Indonesian army[1]. An international peacekeeping force intervened and liberated East Timor. But the tiny half-island nation hardly has any economic means and poverty as well as violence continue to block progress since its official independence in 2002.[2]

The precedent of East Timor encouraged separatist groups in other parts of Indonesia now to increase their demands for independence. Aceh, a small area on the northern tip of Sumatra was an independent sultanate in the 19th century, prior to colonial rule, but was occupied by the Dutch along with Indonesia. Post Indonesian independence it naturally became an Indonesian province. A staunchly Muslim region with a strong sense of identity, it had been dissatisfied with Indonesian secularist leadership. Further it also had oil and gas natural resources which it did not want to share with other provinces. During the 1970s an armed separatist group began fighting for Aceh's independence which, too, was suppressed. Post East Timorese independence, Aceh stepped up its demands for secession and started an armed conflict. At this stage there was a lot of talk about the potential disin-

---

1 History of Timor — Leste, Background Note, 12 Feb 2010, US Department of State, http://www.state.gov/r/pa/ei/bgn/35878.htm
2 Timor-Leste, UN Admits Newest Member State, 27 Sept 2002, UN News Center, http://www.un.org/apps/news/infocusRel.asp?infocusID=27&Body=timor&Body1 =

tegration[1] of Indonesia and it was even compared to Yugoslavia. In general, religious fundamentalism and violence had also crept into the society since a turn to multi party democracy in 1999. However a natural disaster altered this course for a while. In 2004, a massive tsunami struck Indonesia and the warring region, Aceh, being closest to the epicenter, suffered massive casualties. At this time, it benefited greatly from international as well as Indonesian relief programs and the province realized the value of its depen-dence on Indonesia. In 2005 the separatists agreed to give up arms as well as demands for independence in return for greater autonomy as well as con-trol over much of its oil and gas resources. Even so, the Aceh independence movement has ebbed but not disappeared.[2]

If we look at East Timor and Aceh together, it emerges that East Timor was one with West Timor before colonial rule but colonial powers split it up. East Timor highlighted the colonial part of its history to justify separat-ism. In the case of Aceh, it was a separate region before colonial powers took over and integrated it with the Indonesian colony. So it wants to high-light the pre colonial part of its history to justify separatism. It seems like a convenient manipulation of history to serve the apparent common goal in both cases—political opportunism. Likewise, trouble restarted in Papua, where separatists demanded independence in the 1960s but the movement had been crushed. The simmering conflict took an active form[3] post East Timorese independence. Here too, a special package was worked out to grant the province more autonomy as well as the right to retain most of the revenues generated from its natural resources. This pacified the province but some Papuans continue to demand nothing less than an independence referendum.

The Moluccas, Sulawesi, Kalimantan etc., were some other separatist movements that arose but were dampened a little as both Aceh and Papua were not allowed to secede. Other than such separatist movements, reli-gious violence and fundamentalism have also been on the rise. Starting with 2002 Bali bombings, terror attacks have continued and Indonesia also expe-

---

1 Separatism in Indonesia, The Cases of Aceh and Papua, Osamu Inoue, talks about likely disintegration of Indonesia, http://www.jaas.or.jp/pdf/47-4/summary.pdf
2 Aceh: GAM Party Sparks New Round of Anti-Separatist Rhetoric, James Balows-ki, 19 Jul 2007, Green Left, http://www.greenleft.org.au/node/37979
3 New Violence in Indonesia Over Papuan Independence, Bramantyo Prijosusilo, 17 Aug 2008, New America Media, http://news.newamericamedia.org/news/view_article.html?article_id=a72964c40d44d5af7f80bfa9a489leef

rienced sectarian violence for the first time between Christian and Muslim groups. The nation that had held together, modernized and remained secular in an authoritarian rule has become unstable and fractious since its turn to democracy.

Most secessionist movements also become self fulfilling prophecies. The separatists usually carry out militant strikes which the state opposes and suppresses. Violence goes up and the community finally does become oppressed, further justifying the cause of secession. This has been the case in Indonesia, Sri Lanka, Myanmar, and India. Further, allowing secession in one region tends to have a cascading effect on others. By forces of nature, somehow Indonesia escaped disintegration but its stability remains tenuous.[1] If international support for secession and mollycoddling of separatist groups continues, it will threaten the stability of many diverse nations like Indonesia.

THE UN CHARTER: THE RIGHT TO SELF DETERMINATION

The right to self determination featured prominently in the main instruments concerning human rights, the UN charter of 1945 as well as the two international covenants on civil and political rights. Both read, "All peoples have the right of self determination. By virtue of that right, they freely determine their political status and freely pursue their economic, social and cultural development." This principle of self determination held tremendous value post World War II in helping nations achieve independence from colonial rule. Validated by such support, between 1946 and 1960, peoples of 37 new nations freed themselves from colonial rule in Asia, Africa and the Middle East.[2]

However, since the 1990s, continuing international support for self determination has led to an increasing number of conflicts within states as sub groups seek greater autonomy and even full secession. While there is increasing realization of the humanitarian cost of such divisions post bitter experiences in Yugoslavia, Indonesia, etc., there is lack of political will to really change the principle. Since we propagate a near blind belief in people

---

1   Falling Apart, Ron Gluckman, http://www.gluckman.com/IndoYugo.html

Not the Next Yugoslavia: Prospects for the Disintegration of Indonesia, Robert Cribb, 2 Jul 1999, p 169-178, Australian Journal of International Affairs,

2   Understanding Self Determination: The Basics, Karen Parker, Aug 2000, United Nations, http://www.guidetoaction.org/parker/selfdet.html

power, international pressure bodies do not quite know how to disregard a referendum. We continue supporting the archaic principle which seemed valid in a different political context. The empires of the era bygone were expansionist in nature, but democracies of today are inherently secessionist. On this account countless civil wars and armed rebellions are being fought across nations, threatening their stability and peace. Not only do such movements breed chaos and violence in the parent nation but they also reduce the life of a common citizen in the separatist region to utter misery. By the time this region even achieves its independence, the entire infrastructure, economy as well as law and order would be destroyed. Rarely have such states stabilized or prospered after independence.

The status of minorities, especially in a democracy, is an important issue. Any trampling of their rights ought to receive the due media and international groups' attention, as is the case even at present. But the solution isn't the splintering of nations into an ever increasing number of micro nations. That brings the attendant problems of civil wars like ethnic cleansing and the creation of refugees. Further, in the newly independent state, a new minority is created who may have the same insecurities. Secession tends to set off a chain reaction, sometimes disintegrating a whole nation. Its bloody aftermath is often no less disastrous than an expansionist war. In the end it neither serves the majority nor the minority community in a nation. Its key benefactors are the political opportunists who help ferment it.

The charter on "right to self determination" has served its original purpose but continuing with it in principle or on paper is proving detrimental to nations that struggle with diversity. The charter has run its course and ideally should be repealed for greater harmony in the world. If there are any regions that still deserve separation, they should be treated as independent conflicts to be reviewed on a case by case basis. But secession should only be the last resort, saved for rarest of cases, not a standing solution for all communal conflicts of interest, which through this charter it today is. In its current form it is only furthering stealthy political opportunism and militancy as a means of dealing with diversity and differences. In the rising era of people power, some responsibility should be demanded of people, both minorities and majorities, to harmonize and integrate through looking for common ground rather than focusing only on points of difference. This rising communal consciousness and rigid intolerance of differences, which seems to be the case in most diverse democracies today, ought to be condemned and curbed not encouraged.

CHAPTER 7. COALITION GOVERNMENTS: TOO MANY COOKS

In countries with multiple parties, a government may be formed in several ways. If one party wins over 50% of the national vote, it can form a Majority Government. When no single party commands a majority, parties negotiate to form coalitions and together form the government. Alternately, a party may just form a minority government with less than 50% seats but with outside support from some other parties. The process of negotiation between rival parties at times takes several months before a government is formed. Typically, after being in power for a year or two, disagreements emerge between coalition partners and the parliament is dissolved, calling for pre term elections. And the whole process is repeated again. Barring a few nations like the US and the UK, which traditionally have been dominated by a two-party system, most nations round the world today have coalition governments. Even the UK formed one following the 2010 election.

A key factor that results in coalition governments is the method of vote counting. There are two predominant models—Proportional Representation (PR), or the winner takes all (the "First Past the Post"— FPTP model[1].

---

[1] There are two methods of vote counting: A nation is divided into several constituencies which approximates the number of seats in the parliament. In the "winner takes all" or First Past the Post (FPTP) method, a party or candidate winning a plurality of votes in a constituency is declared the winner. In the Proportional Representation (PR) method, votes across constituencies are first aggregated at the national level and winners are declared based on the overall % of votes. There

While the former necessarily leads to coalition governments, even under the latter model coalition and minority governments are possible as is the case in India and Canada.

A common factor across coalition governments has been that they tend to fall too often. A study[1] of nine West European nations like Italy, Denmark and Belgium revealed they had 20 to 46 governments in the 50-year period from 1945–1995. The average number of days a government lasted in the above sample was 611 days, less than two years, roughly half the nominal term. Yet proponents of pluralistic democracy say this form is more democratic, allowing a political platform for divergent ideologies. Some of the coalition governments in nations like Denmark and Switzerland have been considered better than single party rules. Let us examine different coalition governments to assess how they function in reality and what factors drive them towards success or failure in the coalition drama.

Before assessing coalitions, let us take a step back and assess how much deliberative decision-making is already a part of democracy. One often hears people saying that if they were to become the Prime Minister or the President, they would transform the country in a number of ways, maybe rout corruption, improve law and order, clean up the environment, or build infrastructure. These are well meaning but naïve statements. What they mean is that if they became absolute kings, they have thoughts on how they could reform the country. Democracy politicians simply do not hold that degree of power to push through their agendas, no matter how good for the society at large. Democracy is fundamentally a decentralized form of government where power is diffused. Every government decision, small or big, has to be approved by a multitude of stakeholders. A premier and his cabinet have to earn the support of the entire parliament in most decisions. The MPs represent divergent constituencies and on that basis alone often have legitimate conflicting interests. Further, the central government shares power with the state governments, which have their own disparate agendas. Not only does the government have to face elections every 3–5 years, during the term also public opinion is voiced, and shaped, quite strongly by media and activists which are important stakeholders. This government though discus-

---

are several variations of the model. PR model invariably leads to plurality of parties and a coalition government.

1 Coalition Governments and Comparative Constitutional Design, Daniel Diermeier, Hülya Eraslan and Antonio Merlo, Sept 2001, http://www.kellogg.northwestern.edu/faculty/diermeier/papers/eea9-01.pdf

sion and agreement does lead to a slower pace of decision making as well as implementation. Policies take a long time to be formulated through forever unwinding discussions aimed at accommodating the most stakeholders. As a result, a Democratic government is the most checked form of governance but also the weakest. Needless to say, coalition governments add further stakeholders to this deliberative decision making process, further weakening the government. Let us see how they impact governance and also how can they be made to work.

ITALY—IMMOBILISMO

Post World War II, Italy became a democratic republic with PR-based vote counting and an electoral term of 5 years. Since then, Italy has had 61 governments, averaging a little over a year per government term. The reason governments fell usually was on account of smaller partners exercising undue power by constantly withdrawing support or passing no confidence motions over petty issues. For instance the government of Romano Prodi fell in 2007. At the time, Justice Minister Clement Mastella and his wife were being investigated in a corruption case. As leader of a minor party, he abruptly withdrew support for Prodi's coalition as he wasn't getting enough political backing in fighting the corruption case[1]. He cast one of the two votes that brought down Prodi's nine-month-old government.

The frivolity of coalition politics is also evident in the fact that for the first 46 years, nearly every coalition was headed by the dominant Christian Democratic Party. They came to power again and again in coalitions with ever changing partners which included Socialists, Republicans, Democratic Socialists, Liberals and a number of independents and minor parties. These coalitions usually comprised divergent elements from left, right and center with mutually exclusive ideologies. In parliament they often haggled, filibustered and squabbled in bickering inaction which came to acquire a name, *immobilismo*,[2] or do-nothing-ism, right in the 1950s.

---

1 An Italian Government Falls, Again, Gail Edmondson and Court-ney Walsh, 22 Feb 2007, Bloomberg Business Week, http://www.businessweek.com/globalbiz/content/feb2007/gb20070222_938851.htm?chan=top+news_top+news+index_global+business
2 Italy : Immobilismo, 20 Dec 1954, Time, http://www.time.com/time/magazine/article/0,9171,821016,00.html

While the Christian Democrats' continued presence provided some kind of continuity to basic policies like market reform, Italy slowly and steadily slipped into chaos. In the North it led to regionalization of politics which created alienation from the rest of Italy. The South which had always been poor and rural even at the time of democratic reforms suffered even more. In the late 19th century, the Sicilian criminal society or the mafia had come up in these parts. In the fascist era of the early 20th century, Mussolini's autocratic regime initiated a campaign to destroy the mafia. It cracked down on the mafia and their political allies by massive round ups and arrests. By World War II, the mafia hardly existed anymore, as the Sicilian criminal formations had been broken up and neutered. Many Mafiosi fled to the US in this period. Post World War II, following the return to characteristic fluid democracy, the criminal elements returned. With continually changing coalition governments further weakening the federal control, the mafia grew from strength to strength and over time developed a corrupt nexus with the political parties. The money invested in the South to rebuild Sicily led to a construction boom which the mafia monopolized. Some amount of criminal influence also spread to the North. But at the time of democratization, the North was already better developed and industrialized so Italy had far better democracy there than in the South.

Deeply entrenched in criminal influence on politics, corruption, massive debt and general political paralysis led to a total shake up of the system in the early 1990s. All the political parties were caught up in a major scandal called the *Tangentopoli*.[1] All the old parties including the Christian Democrats as well as the Socialist parties ceased to exist. In 1993, some electoral changes were introduced, like the additional member system, though the reforms did not go far enough. Post 1994, leaving their past behind, voters looked forward to a new era which ironically brought Silvio Berlusconi to the center of Italy's politics. Soon Italy went back to having coalition governments whose stability was only marginally better than before. In 1994 itself, Berlusconi's first government fell within months of formation when the Lega Norda withdrew support. However Berlusconi soon entrenched himself deeply in Italian politics and using his media muscle and Machiavellian tactics[2] brought a little more stability, though he remains a polarizing

---

1 "The Sleaze Factor: Clean-Hands Team Fails to Wash Away 'Tangentopoli' Dirt," Fiona Leney, 25 Oct 1994, *The Independent*.

2 "Berlusconi's Long Shadow Casts a Chill Over Italian Politics," Ian Fisher and Elisabetta Povoledo, 2 Feb 2008, *The New York Times*, http://www.nytimes.

figure in Italy and needless to say round the world. Still, he was the first ever Italian prime minister to complete a term between 2001 and 2006, although even that was in two different coalitions. Not much has improved since the supposed reforms. This again shows how, in our singular zeal to only promote democracy, its structural weaknesses in the contemporary context remain unaddressed. Despite Italian voters' demand for a more stable and accountable version of parliamentary democracy, there were no clear cut guidelines for how to achieve that in Italy.

The *immobilismo* that continues to plague Italy manifests itself in different ways. For instance, Naples, a southern city, descended into an unprecedented garbage crisis in 2007. While the dumps had been overflowing beyond capacity, the pleas for more facilities fell on deaf ears. Having exhausted all room for trash at dumps, the collectors stopped picking up garbage in December 2007. Refuse started piling up in the streets and outside people's houses. Lanes and roads became a tapestry of garbage, stink and rodents, and the news even hit international headlines. Goaded by ridicule and embarrassment within and without, PM Prodi announced a series of long and short term measures. Plans were announced to build the much needed incinerators and deploy the Italian army to remove trash piles from the streets of Naples. But before the crisis plan could be executed, Prodi's government fell. It took some time for a new government to form, which later in 2008 put together a hasty patch up solution. The crisis will keep recurring as it has in the past. Incidentally, such garbage crises are common in most developing countries, though it is never called a crisis.

In Italy, democracy seems infinitely weakened or almost paralyzed by the phenomenon of coalition politics.

BELGIUM BLUES—"VELVET DIVORCE" ON ITS MIND

In 2007, a Belgian teacher put up an ad on eBay selling Belgium,[1] offering free delivery but with a qualification that the country was coming secondhand and loaded with debt. This was just one citizen's attempt at drawing attention to the divisive politics and the resultant stalemate in Belgium post-June 2007 elections.

---

com/2008/02/02/world/europe/02italy.html?_r=2

1 "Disgruntled Voter Puts Belgium on eBay," 19 Sept 2007, *USA Today*, http://www.usatoday.com/tech/news/2007-09-18-belgium-ebay_N.htm

An independent nation since 1830, Belgium is a small country with a population of just about 11 million. It has two dominant linguistic groups, the Dutch speaking Flemish in the North and the French speaking Walloons in the south. While a federal structure has stabilized the nation, over time politics has become fiercely regional. Political parties are organized along communal lines and there are no representative parties active in both linguistic communities. Even in Brussels, parties are either exclusively French or Dutch speaking. As in politics, in the society too communal fissures have deepened in the last few decades. Both sides bicker constantly and try to hold on to their linguistic identity, often bringing draconian property and education laws: if you don't speak their language, you cannot buy property or gain admission into schools. The Flemish region, comprising about 60% of the population, has industrialized faster and is doing better economically. Walloons on the other hand once were more powerful both politically and economically, but over time the economy of this region has lagged behind. The North has been demanding greater autonomy and the two sides often come into conflict on linguistic questions in Brussels, which has both the communities.

The coalition governments have grown particularly belligerent and unstable in Belgium. The June 2007 election created a deadlock as it threw up a spate of political parties who could not agree on any coalition arrangement. Unable to come to terms, Belgian politicians started discussing a divorce along Czechoslovakian lines. The impasse lasted over nine months[1] when finally a fragile coalition government was formed in March 2008 under Flemish Prime Minister Yves Leterme. Proving the skeptics true, this government lasted just till the end of the year when Prime Minister Ives Leterme resigned over a financial bailout scandal. However the same coalition continued, now under a new leader, Van Rompuy. He presided over this rambunctious parliament and held it together though he was criticized for do-nothing-ism. While this ensured peace for about a year, Rompuy was elected to European Council presidency and Leterme returned once again in November 2009. Within four months, the government collapsed after the Flemish Liberal party, VLD, withdrew support from the coalition in a row over a linguistic conflict in a part of Brussels.

---

1 "Belgium's No Government Blues," Leo Cendrowicz, 14 Sept 2007, *Time*, http://www.time.com/time/world/article/0,8599,1661965,00.html

Tired of deadlocks, incessant wrangling and political bickering, people voted for a separatist party, the New Flemish Alliance (NVA), in the June 2010 elections.[1] NVA was formed relatively recently, in 2001, with the stated goal of peaceful secession of Flanders from Belgium. From a negligible presence earlier, it now became the largest party with 17.4% of the national vote. If there was political stalemate with Christian Democrats earlier who were only for greater autonomy, the political bickering is only going to get worse now with a party that is demanding secession. In the meantime Belgium faces an economic crisis and its debt to GDP ratio is behind only Greece and Italy in the Eurozone. It remains to be seen how long the uncertainty over the formation of a coalition government will continue this time. Also, since a secessionist party has got plurality of votes, is Belgium headed for a split? While Walloons and Flanders are already like two separate nations, Brussels has a mix of both communities and its future will hang in balance if Belgium does take the extreme step.

The key issue in Belgium's fractious power spats is the fierce split of political parties along linguistic lines. Dutch-speaking parties exist in Flanders and French-speaking in Wallonia; there are no representative parties active in both linguistic regions. Even in Brussels, parties are either exclusively French or Dutch speaking. Thus, they target two separate groups and campaign along mutually exclusive platforms often at odds with the other community. Post elections they are then somehow expected to come together and run a government, which they cannot, lacking in any confluence of goals. A linguistically divided society elects a similarly divided political party which in turn builds loyalty by deepening those divides and the cycle goes on. The crucial issue is not age old existing linguistic differences in the society but how parties have been allowed to form along communal lines making emergent fractures inevitable. United since 1831, Belgium lived in harmony for close to two centuries. Before 2007, polls showed a majority of the population was against a split. However a year down the line post the coalitions' political wrangling, this percentage went up sharply and by the next elections in 2010, a separatist party got the highest vote. Coalition governments of such divergent parties with no common ground whatsoever seem not only to lead to do-nothing-ism but also threaten national unity and stability. Mechanisms are needed to disallow political parties' forma-

---

1 Belgium's Flemish Separatists Make Big Election Gains, 14 Jun 2010, BBC News, http://www.bbc.co.uk/news/10303179

tion along sectarian lines as well as ways to make national governments have a pan national presence.

Having looked at two examples of failed coalition governments, let us look at two successful examples—Denmark and Germany. First, let us take a look at Denmark, often touted as an example of how consensus driven coalition government is superior to single party governments.

DENMARK—"GREEN" AND HAPPY

As in Belgium, in Denmark coalition governments are the norm. In the earlier stated sample period of 1945–1995, Belgium had 34 governments but Denmark was not far behind with 30. Yet the resultant governance and coalition amicability is vastly different. Denmark's coalition governments have been admired for their unique consensual decision making, often even touted to be superior to single party rules. Denmark is a nation that ranks high on the Human Development Index and per capita income and one of the lowest on Income Inequality. In various surveys, it has often won the top slot in being the happiest nation, the most peaceful one, the best business environment and one of the least corrupt in the world, etc. It has been at the forefront of committed environment friendly development since the 1970s. Why? What is it about Denmark's politics that sets it apart?

Since the early 20th century, the Social Democrats (SDP) dominated the political landscape of Denmark. During this period the SDP shared power with several small and minor parties under varied coalitions. SDP led most Danish governments from the 1930s to the early 1980s. The 1970s oil crisis and global slowdown affected Denmark deeply as inflation and unemployment rose and the economy slowed down. This period, especially till 1984, saw a series of frequently falling governments, several of them formed by the SDP. While some of its reform bills were blocked by coalition partners, due to the SDP's almost certain continuity under varying coalitions, long term programs were not abandoned even during economic slowdown. In 1979, the Danish parliament voted to underwrite 30% of the initial cost of wind farms. A decade later these subsidies were dropped but the program had already kicked into a high gear. Today Denmark draws 20% of its electricity from wind energy. Likewise, new homes were designed to be twice as energy efficient and waste heat from local power plants was used to heat

Denmark's houses and offices.[1] While governments like the US were subsidizing fuel in this era, Denmark raised taxes on new cars and motor fuel and encouraged alternate modes of transport. All this energy saving paid off in the long term, making Denmark one of the forerunners on environment protection.

Today the Danes use only half as much energy per capita as many other developed nations like the US. The initiatives that have borne fruit today were undertaken two decades back. This kind of long term management is entirely absent from most democracies with single party governments that last a term or two. Due to presence of coalitions in Denmark where the lead party remained the same and only the coalition partners varied, governance seemed more long term. In Denmark's context therefore it is right to assume that coalition governance has led to better decision making such that policies and directions were not reversed by the next government (as often happens in single party governments). Also, the circus of term to term blaming of the previous government was kept to a minimum as the ruling SDP was virtually always in power, providing continuity as well as ownership of decisions.

Only in the 1990s the political landscape changed when the power dynamic shifted towards center right as Conservatives and Liberals came to power in varying coalitions. However these coalitions also seemed consensual. A vigorous anti inflationary policy was put in place and deficit & debt brought under control. This along with better global economic environment put the Danish economy back on track. At this time, Denmark was plagued by unskilled labor immigration from war torn regions like Yugoslavia and Sri Lanka but it was promptly curbed through appropriate legislation in 2000.

Overall, noteworthy is the fact that throughout its long history of coalition politics, Denmark has had relatively smooth decision making. The differences tend to be sorted out through consensus building approach and the policies seem consistent and long term. To assess why, let us look at the demographics first. Denmark is one of Europe's oldest continuous kingdoms and has gone on almost uninterrupted since the Vikings founded it more than 1100 years ago. Of Denmark's small population base of 5.4 mil-

---

1 Green and Prosperous, Denmark Leads the Way, Philip Warburg, 14 Dec 2009, Boston.com, http://www.boston.com/bostonglobe/editorial_opinion/oped/articles/2009/12/14/green_and_prosperous_denmark_leads_the_way/

lion, 90.5% is of Danish descent and 80.9% of the people are members of the Lutheran state church. Like the rest of Scandinavia, the Danes are only moderately religious, with low levels of church attendance. There are no linguistic, regional or religious divisions. The lack of conflict in the society is what is mirrored in the lack of serious conflict in the parliament. The political parties do not cater to different segments of people. All parties are national in character and there is high degree of confluence of goals, thereby the governments address the problems that the nation is undergoing as a whole at a point of time. Denmark's unique smooth-riding coalition is much more a result of its homogenous civil society than its brand of politics. Its famous consensual coalition politics stems from a natural synergy. The parties do no cater to different population segments and thus have no inherently conflicting and mutually exclusive goals.

Denmark does not have a unique political system but a unique society with a homogenous demographic profile and continuous historic identity that very few nations in the world enjoy. Lifting this model and force fitting it to larger and diverse nations would not lead to similar consensual decision making. Switzerland, another homogeneous nation with continued historical identity, has a similarly amicable coalition in place with consensual decision making. But overall, the dynamics at play here emanate from their unique homogeneous societies and as such may not be scalable to large, complex and heterogeneous nations that by definition will struggle with sharply conflicting goals and interest groups.

There is a coalition model that is scalable—that of a large nation with a checkered history and diverse regions: Germany.

GERMANY—THE QUIET PIONEER

Germany is a large nation with ample scope for division especially after the reunification of East Germany with the highly developed West Germany. The reunification in 1990 was a landmark event that created many socio-economic problems due to the residual diversity of the two lands. However national parties with a pan national presence continued to dominate German politics. Germany follows the PR model and has political plurality but that has never led to regional divisions and splintering of the national mandate[1]. In post World War II Germany, the early decades were dominated by a single party, the Christian Democratic Union (CDU), which ruled in varying coalitions; but unlike most other nations, here the governments were stable and usually lasted full terms. This trend continued when the Social Democrats ruled from 1969 to early 1980s. In 1982 Helmut Kohl of the CDU became the chancellor and his tenure lasted 16 years. During this period, the nation underwent tremendous changes as the Berlin Wall fell in 1990 and East and West Germany were united for the first time since World War II. Kohl's government oversaw the merger and started the process of smoothing over the vast economic and social differences. His government remained popular in East Germany. The 1998 elections brought the SDP back to power and they stayed for two terms. Likewise Angela Merkel's chancellorship that followed has lasted for at least two terms and the second term is still going on in 2010. Germany seems to have far more stability and confluence in its politics. Why? What sets Germany apart?

Germany was first united in 1871 when a federal structure was created to unify its diverse provinces. Post World War I, Germany established a parliamentary republic known as the Weimar Republic. The constitution was weak and that led to frequently falling governments, instability and the rise of extremist parties like the Nazis. Post World War II the nation was split into East and West Germany, which were finally reunified in 1990. Germany's role in the two world wars, the break-up of the nation into halves aligned with the Cold War powers, and the subsequent re-merger clearly marks it as a nation with a very troubled modern history. It also has a significant proportion of international migrants. As per 2004 data, 19% of country's residents were of foreign or partially foreign descent. The unification of almost bipolar East and West Germany has few parallels in the last century. Clearly it is not a case of demographics or inherent unity that is driving Germany's uniquely cohesive and coherent brand of politics. To the contrary, its strengths emanate from its disturbed past. Its pre war Weimar constitution had led to a disaster of international scale and this time round, Germany's constitutional framework, the Basic Law, was crafted in a most diligent and pragmatic manner in 1949. The republic set about the task of creating systems that would never again allow political fragmentation and rise of extremist parties. A crucial minimal threshold clause was adopted

---

1 Analysis: German Coalition Deal, William Horsley, 15 Nov 2005, BBC News, http://news.bbc.co.uk/2/hi/europe/4438212.stm

under which a party must receive at least 5% of the national vote or 3 con-stituency seats in order to get any representation in the *Bundestag*[1]. This was to prevent proliferation of small extremist parties like the ones that desta-bilized and hijacked the Weimar Republic. This electoral hurdle, while it sounds small, had a big impact on the emergent political landscape. It con-solidated power amidst medium and large parties and limited the ascent of fringe issues based small or minor parties. It also prevented regionalization of parties. Further, Germany crafted a positive vote of confidence clause, whereby a government could only be dissolved if an alternate party or coali-tion could prove a majority. Thus the smaller coalition partners could not play kingmakers over minor issues and make governments fall as they do, with regularity, in Italy or India. In Germany, since 1949, only 2 such votes of confidence have been attempted and of that only one was successful. If a coalition partner withdraws support but cannot prove an alternate major-ity, the government completes its full term, now as a minority government.

As a result, Germany has two major parties, the Social Democratic Party (SDP) and the Christian Democratic Union along with its sister party, the Christian Social Union (CDU/CSU). It further has three main smaller par-ties, the Free Democratic Party, the Left and the Greens alliance. These par-ties have a pan national presence and agenda and differ mainly in terms of political ideology.[2] The SDP, as elsewhere in Europe, is a center-left party, believing in a social market economy. The CDU is a conservative party be-lieving in a dominant role for the market but advocating state intervention to prevent social hardships. The CSU (more to CDU's right) has a presence only in Bavaria but it is more or less fused with the latter. The Greens are a loose coalition of environment focus groups. The FDP comprises liberals who advocate free market economics and reduced government intervention.

Of particular interest in this discussion is the emerging Left party. One of its coalition partners, the PDS, is the successor to East Germany's com-munist party. The PDS's base remains East Germany, where it can garner up to one fifth of the voters, compared to only about 1% in West Germany. It failed to cross the minimum 5% of national vote threshold in the 2002 elections even though it won the required three constituencies. To broad-en its base and become a national party, in 2007 it formed a coalition with

---

1 Electoral System in Germany, German Culture, http://www.germanculture.com. ua/library/facts/bl_electoral_system.htm

2 Germany's Political parties, 6 Sept 2005, BBC News, http://news.bbc.co.uk/2/hi/ europe/4219274.stm

the WASG party. This coalition gained a presence in Western Germany in Lower Saxony, Hesse and Hamburg. Germany's cutoff rule requiring 5% of the national vote thus pushed its parties to pursue a pan-national presence. As a result there is a predominance of large parties that are differentiated by ideology and not vote blocs. Far right parties like the neo Nazis, NDP and DVU enjoyed some success in select provinces but were stifled as they fell short of the required 5% of the national vote. This is exactly what the Basic Law had aimed to achieve.

This minimum cut-off clause exists in most Western European nations and has also been instituted in some of the Eastern European neo democracies. Poland faced the mushrooming of several small interest-group parties when it turned to democracy. Prior to the 1993 elections, it undertook reforms and adopted the minimum 5% cutoff clause for parties to gain representation in the parliament. It further improvised by making the cutoff slightly higher, at 8%, for coalitions. As a result it was able to axe all the minor and divisive parties and only six parties gained representation in the parliament.

Further, Germany has a federal system which goes beyond power sharing between center and states to also sharing resources between states. The decade after reunification, for instance, was a crucial period for Germany. While it was an emotional reunion to begin with, it brought deep social problems in its wake. The dismantling of old systems and structures in East Germany led to housing shortages, unemployment and increases in crime and right wing violence. Helmut Kohl's government responded with alacrity; security was tightened and violence brought under control. At the same time, West Germany transferred large sums of money towards the development of East Germany. This led to deficit budgets for the whole, but the principle of unity and genuine federalism was sustained. This further discouraged regionalization as people in East Germany came to identify with the national government.

While Germany has a pluralistic democracy, it has stability and focus while staying large. It is a powerful nation and its stability has influenced the entire region and has been crucial in giving Europe leverage in the global scenario. Size and unity do help. Its minimum threshold, a positive vote of confidence, and shared federalism have been instrumental to Germany's unified and stable politics.

ADDITIONAL CONSIDERATIONS REGARDING COALITION GOVERNMENTS

Environmental Movement and Coalitions

Environmental groups are one of the ardent champions of coalition governance and pluralistic democracy. Let us briefly assess what impact they have had so far through the mechanism of coalitions.

In Germany, the Greens have been in existence since 1980 but shared power for the first time in 1998 with the SDP under Gerhard Schröder in what was called as the Red–Green coalition. As a partner in this coalition, the Greens were able to negotiate an agreement to start phasing out civilian nuclear plants. Nuclear energy accounted for 30% of Germany's energy needs at the time. The conservatives opposed the plan as alternative sources of energy had not been identified or developed and overdependence on oil was adding budgetary burden. They even pledged to reverse it when they come back to power. Greens also came under criticism from their own voters as in bargain for phasing out nuclear energy, the Greens had agreed to sending troops to Afghanistan that went counter to the agenda voters had mandated them. This Red–Green coalition ended in 2005 and the next coalition government did not include the Greens. The nuclear phasing out that had been negotiated remained nebulous on timeline. Lacking true political will, its implementation has been tardy.

A far more lasting and sustained environment movement took place in the Scandinavian countries Sweden and Denmark, where the mainstream parties like the Social Democrats championed the cause. The Greens never gained any parliamentary support in those nations. As per Euro-barometer, regular surveys carried out by EC in the 1970s showed nations like Denmark and Sweden were among the most environmentally conscience countries in Europe. Environment would be part of people's living room discussions and a lot of grassroots movements like car free Sundays were initiated. Again, as the demos, so the democracy! Thus for a movement like environmentalism to succeed, it needs coming together of public and political will. It remains to be seen if environmental groups or parties can truly influence the movement as smaller coalition partners.

Overall, coalitions and pluralistic democracy are harder work but have been supported for being more democratic. For instance it has been said that there is room for alternate ideologies than just two platforms that two party systems offer. There is some truth in that but in reality, even in nations dominated by two large parties, the parties are not rigid but constantly changing forms. Party ideologies and campaign platforms have evolved substantially over time keeping in line with emergent issues. In most coalitions, smaller partners often exercise larger influence than mandated to them which could be called less democratic. Many of the coalition governments typically also lack transparency as divergent parties have different manifestos and no genuine agreement is reached. Governance then becomes a succession of back room deals and vote buying exercise. While the debate between twin party system versus pluralistic democracy may still go on based on what vision experts have on democracy. But for our practical purpose, especially in the context of developing nations, let us see what we have distilled from an analysis of the hits and misses of coalition politics.

Minimum Threshold—Relevance

Romania turned to democracy after the fall of communism in 1989. In a nation of just over 20 million, about 200 political parties sprang up, most revolving around personalities rather than programs. Many of these parties represented small regional or ethnic groups and they could only form coalition governments, usually made up of a large number of parties, which were querulous and unstable. The first decade of democracy witnessed about seven prime ministers coming and going. Post this shaky start, however, some reforms were undertaken to make it more similar to the German system. At first a 3% threshold was adopted, which was raised to 5% for parties and 8–10% for cartels. This brought the number of parties down to about five or six and democracy stabilized in the following period.[1]

India started experimenting with coalition governments since 1989, coinciding with the decline of its then largest party Congress. In the three years after the 1996 elections, the government fell five times, albeit three times the same Prime Minister came back in different coalitions. The shortest government spell in this time was 13 days. In most coalitions, smaller partners—small regional parties or independents that can win only a constituency or two—have held up governance decisions over petty issues.

1 Electoral Reforms in Romania, Towards a Majoritarian Electoral System? Jean-Benoit Pilet and Jean-Michel De Waele, *European Electoral Studies*, EVS, http://ispo.fss.muni.cz/uploads/EVS/003/03.pdf

They are known to play kingmakers, blackmailing the larger parties as they can leave a coalition and join the next government that comes to power.

India has the FPTP method of vote counting but there are hundreds of parties and the coalitions usually are made up of as many as 15–20 parties. Indian politics would improve greatly with a minimum cutoff clause that would allow parties with pan-national presence to gain representation in the national parliament. It would also bring down the number of cooks meddling in the coalition soup to 5 or 6 instead of the 15–20 it normally has.

Positive Vote of Confidence

Coalition governments and proportional representation model have been supported on the ground that they are more democratic, reflecting the true diversity in the society.[1] While in theory this is true, in reality they are indeed less democratic. In most nations, the smaller partners usually play the role of a kingmaker and exert greater influence on the decision making process than mandated to them. By instituting a positive vote of confidence measure, Germany ensured that coalition governments are stable and small parties cannot play kingmakers or eternal blackmailers. If this clause had been adopted in the 1994 reforms in the Italian shake up, it would have helped Italy curb its curse of frequently falling and unstable governments where the smaller partners blackmail the larger parties and destabilize its politics. Likewise, in Belgium the smaller partners have withdrawn support over petty issues and brought the nation to its current impasse. In all countries which have coalition governments, positive vote of confidence could be instituted such that, in order to make an existing coalition fall, an alternative must prove its majority appeal. This would ensure that a coalition once formed is stable and the nation is not without a government—the "headless chicken" phase—till the next elections. This would also stop the phenomenon of frequently falling governments that plagues most of Europe and other countries with coalition governments.

Factionalism—The Banal Problem

Whether we study coalitions or secession or fundamentalism, factionalism seems to be the common thread. It is the one corrupting factor that

---

1 Is Coalition Government Preferable to Government by a Single Party? Debate : Coalition Government, Debatepedia, Idea, International Debate Education Association, http://debatepedia.idebate.org/en/index.php/Debate:_Coalition_government

strikes at the root of democracy. The formation of political parties and campaigning along sectarian lines undermines democracy and ought to be curbed through appropriate legislation. In Belgium, if parties had not been allowed to organize along linguistic lines, the voters would have been divided on ideology. Even now, Christian Democrats, Liberals and Socialists have presence in both the communities but each party has two separate entities—one French-speaking and the other Dutch-speaking. Such deep fissures have made coalition governance impossible. This sectarian brand of politics that proliferated in the last few decades has also led to rising intolerance in the two communities and brought a nation that has been in existence since about the 1830s to the brink of dismemberment. From every aspect, now also from the perspective of coalition governance, factionalism in politics where political parties split up the national body politic into sectarian groups ought to be curbed through legislative checks. To allow room for addressing regional interests, a federal structure should be instituted as indeed has been done in most nations. But the national level politics should ideally have a pan national presence and character.

To sum up, in homogeneous nations coalitions may offer good governance as there is a natural confluence of goals. In large heterogeneous nations, coalition governments add a lot of complexity. In order for that to not be disruptive, structural reforms like those discussed above are essential if governance is to be delivered in reality.

CHAPTER 8. WORKADAY FREEDOM: DIFFERENTIAL FREEDOM NEEDS

Freedom of expression has, nowadays, come to mean the entirety of what it is to be free. In reality, people living amidst violence or extreme poverty would hardly consider themselves free even if they had freedom of speech, free elections and free media. Freedom needs to be understood from the citizen's life perspective, based on how free a person really feels. At the first level, people ought to feel free to exist. If there is widespread crime and violence in a society, no one can feel free. Next is economic freedom. People living amidst poverty are helpless and not free, even if they have freedom of speech. Only upon fulfillment of these basic freedom needs does a higher order need like freedom of expression become relevant or meaningful. Let us examine each dimension of freedom and also its relation with democracy.

BASIC LIBERTY—THE FREEDOM TO EXIST

If there is widespread violence in a society, it does not really matter if we have freedom of expression as we are yet to achieve freedom to even exist.

The rule of law is a central tenet of a democratic republic which essentially means that a government rules as per a set of laws. In the context that this was established, aristocratic monarchs and colonial powers ruled the world. It was considered important to curtail authority of the state such that it did not turn into arbitrary rule and instead respected an individual's natural rights. To a large extent this has been achieved in most functional democracies where the state is no longer an unbridled force to be feared. However, it does not automatically lead to good law and order. While people are now free from state sponsored oppression, they have much more to fear from each other. In most developing world democracies, crime and violence have risen multifold after the collapse of authoritarian rule. The focus on "rule of law" has been to check state power but it does not check the equally oppressive tendencies of people power. In authoritarian states, most abuses are committed by the state but in democratic states, most abuses are committed by the people themselves. Most human rights organizations continue to measure human rights abuses based largely on those committed by the state. Only recently, a Global Peace Index has incorporated measures such as level of violent crime and level of distrust in other citizens in its measurement of peace in a nation. Violence or fear of violence in a society is a limiting factor on people's day to day freedom and ought to be measured as such, regardless of who the offender is—state or common criminals. Let us assess some of the democracies on this dimension, as they exist in reality.

Going from the worst to the best:

In 2006, Democratic Republic of Congo approved a new sexual violence law which broadened the definition of rape to also bring sexual harassment, slavery etc. under its purview. So while progress has been made in terms of greater rule of law on paper, the lawlessness in reality continues to spiral downwards at an alarming rate. This is what Tacitus, a senator and historian in ancient Rome, meant when he said the more numerous the laws, the more corrupt the state. Without implementing even basic levels of law, the state here is busy refining laws further. Given the total breakdown of structure and authority in the state, the laws have no meaning. Some degree of authority is essential to maintaining order in a society and bringing in decentralized democracy amidst war in Congo has achieved the opposite effect. Violence has escalated post a turn to democracy in 2006. The state troops sent to protect people are involved in heinous crimes and the common people themselves are busy brutalizing each other.

South Africa has been dubbed the crime capital of the world and also the most dangerous country in the world, which is not at war.[1] While murders, violent robberies etc. are commonplace, women, especially minors, are the

---

1 South Africa Struggles With Crime Rate, Robyn Dixon, 27 Sept 2009, Los Angeles Times, http://articles.latimes.com/2009/sep/27/world/fg-crime-police27

worst sufferers of sexual violence with little recourse to justice or social reconciliation. As said earlier, a woman born in the country has a greater chance of being raped than learning how to read.[1] While this has been blamed on the previous apartheid regime, it is noteworthy that this kind of crime did not exist in that era, which is still no justification for it. Now, South Africa has a functional democracy in place with multiple parties and its elections have been deemed free by international observers. But that does not mean it has liberty. Just placing power in the hands of a hardened and violence prone poor majority does not necessarily liberate them. It could do just the opposite. In South Africa, people's fundamental liberty has been thwarted and everyone, particularly the weakest sections like women and children, stand to be abused, not by state but by the people themselves. South Africa has one of the most progressive constitutions in the world which was debated and crafted over three years. But that has not translated into good law and order or "liberty" in reality. "Rule of Law" by design only ensures that a government operates as per the legislation. It seems to have overlooked the need for tough measures to check abuses by people under the newfound freedom as liberty is murdered at its own hands.

In India, about one in four members elected to the parliament face criminal charges ranging from murder, rapes, extortion, etc. There are many instances of candidates running election campaigns from their jail cells. While they could be blamed for corrupt criminal behavior, these are known facts. People still vote for them provided the candidates promise them something free or play them along divisive lines. India has the world's longest written constitution and the rule of law on paper is detailed, progressive and comprehensive. In fact it is so long and detailed that it has often been alleged that no MP has ever read it. Let us see how it is in practice.

Filing a police complaint requires some degree of influence as it spoils the police record and the police is generally apathetic to crime. Even if a police complaint is registered, due to the politician criminal nexus, evidence is botched up as has happened in several cases involving foreigners and in the mob lynching of a *dalit* family in Khairlanji. The average lifespan of a case in India is 15 years. It is estimated that it would take the judiciary 320 years to clear the backlog of over 30 million cases even though a court spends on an

---

1 South Africa : Rape Facts, 11 May 2010, Dispatches, Channel 4, http://www.channel4.com/programmes/dispatches/articles/south-africa-rape-facts

average just 4 minutes 55 seconds on a case.[1] One of the key reasons for the delay is a rudimentary system and lack of enough sitting judges. The justice ministry called for an increase of 50 judges per million people by 2013 but the government would not be able to pay for such an overhaul. The revenues are instead squandered on freebie schemes as that is the only thing the voters understand and appreciate. India's crime rate is rising and there is almost a near total absence of law and order in rural India, which accounts for 70% of the population. Even in urban India, crimes against women are on the rise. Rape is the fastest growing crime[2] and there are 5,000 dowry deaths per annum where women are murdered, often burnt to death, by in-laws for failing to get more dowry. India has democracy and excellent rule of law on paper. But that does not translate into good law and order or liberty in reality.

The developed nations are doing far better, but even there sharp intra nation differences exist. In the US, youth homicide rates are more than 10 times that of other leading industrial nations and on a par with the rates in some of the fast developing countries. On an average 90,000 rapes[3] are reported in the US every year. This is despite the fact that substantial resources are invested in the policing as well as judiciary system. Every year more than 13 million people enter US prisons and jails, of which 95% will eventually be released.[4]

While the modern legal theory revolves around reformation and rehabilitation, evidence from reality proves to the contrary. It is estimated that most of these criminals leave the prisons angrier and more violent than when they were first incarcerated. Some 6.5 million inmates are released every year, of which two thirds will be re-arrested within three years. The cycle creates new crime victims. The supposedly correctional facilities cost millions of dollars but there is sufficient evidence that they correct nothing

---

1 It'll Take 320 Years to Clear Legal Backlog, TNN, 7 Mar 2010, The Times of India, http://timesofindia.indiatimes.com/india/Itll-take-320-years-to-clear-legal-backlog/articleshow/5652826.cms

2 India's Fastest Growing Crime: Rape and the Fight for Justice, Priyanka Bhardwaj, 22 Mar 2010, The WIP.net, http://www.thewip.net/contributors/2010/03/indias_fastest_growing_crime_r.html

3 Crime in The United States, 1989-2008, US Department of Justice — Federal Bureau of Investigation, Sept 2009, http://www.fbi.gov/ucr/cius2008/data/table_01.html

4 Prison Violence Can Heighten Public Danger, Dan Harris, 7 Jun 2006, ABC News, Good Morning America, http://abcnews.go.com/GMA/LegalCenter/story?id=2048040&page=1

in fact make criminals more violent. The overall crime solving rate in developed nations like the UK is estimated to be about 20%[1] and conviction rates are pathetic. In the UK, the conviction rate for index crimes hovers between 4–14%. In this, out of only about 25% of rape cases that are reported, conviction rate is a meager 5.6%, whereas research suggests only 3–8 % are false allegations. Crime, as is often said today, has become a low risk business and is no wonder it is on the rise.

If there is one thing that could be said of liberty and rule of law in democracy, it would be that they "died of a theory." The reality check seems to be missing and very little attention is being paid to corroborate the theories upon which we have founded our systems. This is not to say that we have to revert to medieval methods but there are ways to solve problems, if we acknowledge them and focus on them. Jack Straw, the UK's former Justice Secretary, urged recognition of the high crime incidence in the society and suggested passing a Human Responsibilities Law[2] to balance human rights. This kind of recognition of the human responsibility angle in a democracy is an important first step. Further, prison reforms have been managed in reality as was done by police officer Kiran Bedi in India's notorious Tihar Jail, for which she received some international awards, but such successes remain localized. Solutions are possible if we focus on problems and only accept theories based on what they achieve in reality.

While all systems other than democracy are summarily dismissed as "not free," let us see how they perform on this basic dimension of individual liberty. The US State Department notes that despite a recent increase in crime, China remains one of the countries with the lowest crime rate in the world.[3] And of the crimes reported, theft accounted for about 80%. Crimes against women and children are particularly low and women seem free to dress as they please and move about at all hours of the day without any significant worries of assault or harassment. From women's point of view,

---

1 Tens of Thousands of CCTV Cameras, Yet 80% of Crime Unsolved, Justin Davenport, 19 Sept 2007, London Evening Standard, http://www.thisislondon.co.uk/news/article-23412867-tens-of-thousands-of-cctv-cameras-yet-80-of-crime-unsolved.do

2 Jack Straw: Human Rights Act Needs Rebalancing, 8 Dec 2008, politics.co.uk, http://www.politics.co.uk/news/opinion-former-index/legal-and-constitutional/jack-straw-human-rights-act-needs-rebalancing-$1253397.htm

3 China, Country Specific Information - Crime, Travel.State.Gov, A Service of the Bureau of Consular Affairs, US Department of State, http://travel.state.gov/travel/cis_pa_tw/cis/cis_1089.html

that is freedom. True, the government does not allow freedom of expression and political activism and these will be discussed also. But it provides for basic freedom needs better than some democracies, as aptly verbalized by the Indian writer Gurcharan Das, who said that India has law and China order.[1] Similarly, smaller nations like Singapore and UAE, which also have unitary rule, have long been considered safe havens almost free of crime and violence. On the other hand, most erstwhile communist states experienced a huge increase in violence post their political opening up. Poland has experienced fourfold increase in violent robberies and crime since 1984. Even the Czech Republic, one of the more homogeneous, prosperous and peaceful of nations, has been overrun with crime and other social ills like money laundering, smuggling, illegal arms trade, prostitution and juvenile delinquency. Democratic reforms in Albania in the early 1990s are also said to have been accompanied by a growth in crime, in part because controls once exercised by the state and police were lifted. Mexico too has faced a rise in illegal drug trafficking and violence coinciding with the fall of its single party regime in 2000.

Yet there is little debate about loss of such a basic freedom under a relatively loosely structured democratic model. Going back in time, the Enlightenment Age thinkers often focused on this aspect. Montesquieu is considered one of the greatest philosophers of liberalism from the Enlightenment era. According to him, political liberty[2] is "a tranquility of mind arising from the opinion each person has of his safety." Liberty is not the freedom to do whatever we want: if we have the freedom to harm others, for instance, others will also have the freedom to harm us, and we will have no confidence in our own safety. Liberty involves living under laws that protect us from harm while leaving us free to do as much as possible, and that enable us to feel the greatest possible confidence that if we obey those laws, the power of the state will not be directed against us. Flowing from this, he emphasized a strong connection between liberty and the details of the criminal law.

In many democracies, the state does not play a directly oppressive role but that does not mean people don't do it to each other. As evidence shows,

---

1 "India Has Law, China Order," Gurcharan Das, 10 Apr 2005, *The Times of India*, http://timesofindia.indiatimes.com/articleshow/1073496.cms

2 Baron de Montesquieu, Charles-Louis de Secondat, 18 Jul 2003, Hilary Bok, *The Stanford Encyclopedia of Philosophy*, Edward N. Zalta, http://plato.stanford.edu/entries/montesquieu/

power placed wrongly in the hands of people have led them to abuse human rights with heinousness unparalleled even among the worst tyrannies. Human rights abuses should be measured regardless of who does it, state or people. In our world today much ado is made about oppression or violence if it is undertaken by a state, which ought to continue but most human rights organizations measure oppression by state or state factors only. The widespread abuse by common people in the form of general crime and violence remains unaccounted for in the data thus produced. Providing or enabling day to day freedom is an important part of good governance as delivered to the citizens. If on an average the risk of exposure to crime and violence and associated fear is high, that is loss of freedom. Taking part in elections or having a free press is no substitute for that. Truth be told, if nations, including the exalted democracies, have high crime rates, they have no business calling themselves free.

FREEDOM FROM POVERTY—AND HELPLESSNESS

There is no freedom like having a little money in your pocket. As also said by Franklin Delano Roosevelt, true individual freedom cannot exist without economic security and independence. People undertake life threatening journeys to reach the US and Europe to escape poverty and lack of economic opportunity not to attain freedom of expression or a right to vote. They don't travel to Ghana or India so they can enjoy freedom of expression. In fact people from these "free" nations go to live and work in Saudi Arabia, leaving the charms of democracy behind. As the World Bank defines it, "Poverty is hunger. Poverty is lack of shelter. Poverty is being sick and not being able to see a doctor. Poverty is not having access to school and not knowing how to read. Poverty is not having a job, is fear for the future, living one day at a time. Poverty is losing a child to illness brought about by unclean water. Poverty is powerlessness, lack of representation and *freedom*." Removal of poverty is essential to restoring basic human dignity and freedom. Over 3 billion people, nearly half the world lives on less than $2.5 a day.[1] Democracy or not, freedom is a distant goal. It has been argued that bringing in democracy automatically eradicates poverty. Let us see if that is true.

---

1 "Poverty Facts and Stats," Anup Shah, 28 Mar 2010, *Global Issues*, http://www.globalissues.org/article/26/poverty-facts-and-stats

Ghana, long considered a model for democracy in Africa, has always been puzzling to experts for what they call the "economic paradox of Ghana's poverty."[1] The nation is largely free of civil strife that plagues many of the African nations. It has a full-fledged multi party democracy where elections are deemed free and power shifts hands peacefully. Ghana has invested heavily in developing a peaceful and functional democracy and earned the world's accolades for doing that. The administration is adjudged to be relatively corruption free and hard working. Yet living standards are only marginally higher than they were decades ago. Its Human Development Index, HDI, at 0.526, is barely over the low development cut off of 0.5 and its rank is a poor 152nd in the world. While it is well endowed with natural resources like gold, the nation's per capita nominal GDP ranks about 140 in the world, similar to nations like Zambia and Bangladesh, with 28% of its population below the poverty line of $1.25 a day.

What is the reason for that? The answer lies in its economic profile. The majority of the population remains dependent on agriculture and manufacturing contributes just 7.9% to Ghana's GDP. The nation has simply failed to industrialize or develop its economy. Its exports remain focused on raw materials rather than value-added goods. Once again, there is no correlation between democracy and economic prosperity. Developing a robust market economy is a must for providing economic liberty to people, which Ghana has not been able to do.

There is a parallel here. An irate Rastafarian noted[2] that "Singapore was similar to Afrikan [sic] blood countries in the 60s, abused, bleeding and brain damaged by the West... yet the servants of that nation have served their people well and let us learn from it." While extremist in sentiment, the example provided couldn't be more apt. Singapore, a poor, ethnically heterogeneous, resource poor and unstable nation in the 1960s has turned around in a remarkably short span of time to be the frontrunner in all measures of economic prosperity. Its per capita GDP ranks fourth in the world. Its HDI is 0.944, reflecting its highly developed status; it has a GDP of $177 billion with a population base of just 5 million. Ghana on the other hand is at $18 billion in GDP with a population base of 24 million. Ghana is being chosen

---

1 "The Economic Paradox of Ghana's Poverty," Michael M. Weinstein, 10 Nov 2003, *Financial Times*, Council on Foreign Relations, http://www.cfr.org/publication/6514/economic_paradox_of_ghanas_poverty.html?id=6514

2 Singapore was like the Afrikan blood countries, Ceska Sankare, 11 Feb 2010, World of Jah, http://www.worldofjah.com

as a benchmark here because it has been adjudged to be the most functional and clean democracy in Africa. It has long been presented as a role model for other African nations to follow. Only recently experts have started wondering why then it still remains poor and backward. Singapore, on the other hand, has managed to develop a world class economy[1] even though it is a single party state. Singapore enjoys a remarkably open and corruption-free environment, stable prices, and a per capita GDP higher than even most developed countries. The economy depends heavily on exports but of manufactured goods and services not raw materials. Further, already a safe state, the minimal crime has shown a further decline[2] of 10% as measured in 2006. An equally strong emphasis is placed on multi-racial harmony, given its experience with racial riots before independence. The government has taken strong measures to control ethnically inspired discrimination in education and employment. To avoid the evolution of racial ghettoes in public housing, all housing projects are required to have a certain percentage of minority population. Citizen and community groups are encouraged to be multi-racial. Despite failing to deliver higher order needs like freedom of expression, Singapore has done remarkably well on delivering basic needs like freedom of peaceful existence and widespread prosperity.

On account of being the most successful and large democracy, India again needs to be highlighted as an example. Due to its large population base of 1.2 billion, the world's largest number of poor and illiterate live in India[3]. While its population below poverty line is estimated to be 26%, similar to other developing countries, in absolute terms, this comprises upwards of 400 million people who are poor, 75% of who live in rural India. When India achieved independence its population below poverty line was 47%. In its turn to a socialist economy with nationalization of industries, this figure actually went up to 56% in 1974. Since the market reforms initiated in 1991, there has been a significant reduction in poverty. So freedom from abject poverty seems linked to good macro-economic management

1 Building Capabilities: The Singapore Success Story, Andrew Jensen, 7 Mar 2010, World Poverty and Human Rights Online, http://wphr.org/2010/andrew-jensen/building-capabilities-the-singapore-success-story/

2 Why Singapore Enjoys A Low Crime Rate: Review, Kishore Mahbubani, 15 Jul 2009, Strait Times, http://www.mahbubani.net/articles%20by%20dean/why%20singapore%20has%20low%20crime%20rate.pdf

3 Poverty in India Since 1974, James W Fox, 29 Nov 2002, Nathan Associates Inc., USAID/ Washington, http://www.ekh.lu.se/ekhcgu/teaching/401d4/poverty%20in%20india.pdf

than mere presence of democracy. But paradoxically, Indian economy remains crippled and is not able to lift itself up to its potential on account of people's opposition to development initiatives as well as infrastructure investments. So in a way democracy stands in the way of liberating people from poverty. Saying that democracy has not proven any correlation with poverty reduction may not entirely be true. It might be possible to prove it indeed has a negative correlation as it slows down development and poverty reduction.

Just like single party Singapore, China too has reduced poverty by an unprecedented scale over the last 20 years. World Bank estimates that its poverty fell from 85% to 15%[1] and nearly 600 million people were "liberated" from poverty between 1981 and 2005. China accounts for most of the reduction in world poverty in the last century. Given that it has good order as well, it is no wonder then that most people claim that they feel free in China today. The democratic world does not understand that and often wonders if they even know the meaning of freedom because in the world view, freedom is equated with freedom to speak. That is a definition more relevant to developed nations' context. In the developing world, people still have not experienced basic freedom like just a daily right to exist without fear of violence or without worries about the next meal for the family. Living amidst destitution, poverty and violence, freedom of thought, speech or association are entirely superfluous.

In the developing world, law and order as well as poverty reduction has been poorer in democratic nations whereas some, not all, of the unitary states have done much better. Maybe some order and structure is required in an elementary society to bring it up to a level where freedom given to people is not subversive. Democracy thus has been deficient in meeting basic freedom needs of the developing world. However it is unparalleled in delivering higher order needs like freedom of expression. In the developed nations, where by and large basic needs are met, this dimension of freedom becomes important to enable true freedom. So as a nation becomes developed, democracy becomes a superior model as it is the only system that meets higher order freedom needs.

---

1   "Poverty Around the World," Anup Shah, 1 Mar 2010, *Global Issues*, http://www.globalissues.org/article/4/poverty-around-the-world#WorldBanksPovertyEstimatesRevised

HIGHER ORDER NEEDS—FREEDOM OF EXPRESSION

As said Einstein, "Everything that is really great and inspiring is created by the individual who can labor in freedom." While the first two kinds of basic freedoms are essential to a basic dignified human existence it is this third dimension of freedom that truly enables a great civilization. Freedom of expression is at the core of all human progress. Democracy has erred on the side of anarchy but man has made revolutionary progress in sciences and arts only under freedom. In ancient times, the Greek democratic period led to breathtaking advancement across fields like medicine, astronomy, philosophy, literature, and science. Post the decline of this civilization and reversal to traditional empires, this slowed down to a trickle and mankind plunged back into the dark ages, so called for their lack of any cultural achievements.

The quest for knowledge and higher ideals was rekindled in Europe during the Renaissance, the Scientific Revolution, and the Age of Enlightenment. These brought about political opening up and freedom of expression, leading to another era of exploration and advancement across an ever expanding field of arts, sciences, and technology. The germ theory of disease, followed by the invention of antibiotics and vaccination, changed human health and lifespan expectations forever. Advances in metallurgy and the development of steam engines and railroads took transportation to a new level, enabling speedy movement of goods and people. Important discoveries were made in astronomy, chemistry, and quantum mechanics. Human psychology was explained, liberating societies from regressive thoughts and practices. The Green revolution made defunct threats of large scale famines that had haunted mankind forever. The 20th century saw a communication revolution with the advent of mass media, telephones, personal computing and internet. Literature, arts and entertainment became widespread pursuits. The list is ever expanding.

It may be worth noting here that the discoveries and inventions in the 19th century, with limited suffrage, were just as significant as those made during the 20th century with its mass democracy. That this suffrage was not inherited but was steadily expanding in line with prosperity might have added a fillip to the entrepreneurial spirit, crucial to advancement. If one aspect of liberty is innovation, another is the presence of a free media that checks governments and nations. Over time, free media and journalism have empowered the quest for truth and promoted greater transparency in governance as well as society. This dimension of liberty has indeed created a higher order civilization.

All other models fall short in this respect. China is an example. The worst phase for Chinese intellectuals was clearly the Mao Zedong era, 1949–1976, when critics were prosecuted, sent to labor camps and sentenced to life in prison or death. People were compelled to praise Mao and his regime. Access to even basic information on other nations was prohibited in this period. However, after 1978, the Chinese government did change substantially. Economic opening up and internet increased the nation's exposure to the outside world and its ideologies. The government continues exercising some censorship and freedom of expression remains limited. But it has changed its strategy of dealing with dissent. As prosecuting revolutionaries catapulted them to hero like status in the society, the government has now adopted a far more covert and sophisticated approach. As economist Qinglian He notes,[1] "Now the government pursues active discrimination at every level of the society. People who 'fall into line' get incentives, career rewards, promotions etc. and those who don't are sidelined and forced into oblivion and unemployment—no one even hears of them." As the nation becomes developed, this kind of a model would have its limitations as it stifles thought and creativity as well as hampering transparency. Even so, this approach is better than the violent mode of many regimes in the world today who suppress dissent through state-sponsored torture and violence. It may sound heretical, but barbaric regimes could switch to the Chinese model such that they are more humane in suppressing political dissent. As compared to the developed nations, however, even this sophisticated stifling of thought and expression is detrimental to freedom in the world.

Lack of freedom of expression in the long run would take us back to the dark ages of unquestioning belief in dogmas and hierarchy. Enabling freedom of expression, innovations and advancements has been one of the proven core strengths of democracy.

---

1 Academic Freedom in China, Qinglian He, May — Jun 2002, Academe Online, American Association of University Professors, http://www.aaup.org/AAUP/pubsres/academe/2002/MJ/Feat/Qing.htm

MEASURES OF FREEDOM

What we measure is what we get. How is freedom measured in our world today and how should it be? Let us briefly assess the present indices used to define this parameter.

The Freedom Index is a yearly report by the US-based Freedom House. A "freedom index" is obtained based on political rights and civil liberties which are rated on a scale of 1 to 7. Based on the composite rating, a nation is declared as Free, Partly Free or Not Free. While seemingly an index of freedom, what it seems to be measuring is the extent of democracy. Nations like South Africa and Indonesia receive a high ranking and are deemed free. All non democratic nations are labeled Not Free. China is rated worse than Afghanistan or the Democratic Republic of Congo. Once again, what is delivered to the citizens is forsaken in favor of a preferred theory and form of governance. From a citizen's point of view, freedom index should ideally define which nation would people feel more free living in. It would be incredulous if any people would feel more free living in Democratic Republic of Congo or Afghanistan vis-à-vis China.

The *Economist* has a similar index but it is rightly called the Democracy Index. Practically every nation calls itself a republic or a democracy; this index is useful in determining how true that is. It examines the state of democracy in terms of five attributes—electoral process and pluralism, civil liberties, functioning of government, political participation and political culture. Countries are then classified into Full Democracies, Flawed Democracies, Hybrid Regimes and Authoritarian Regimes. This is a straightforward and more truthful index that measures exactly what it claims to measure—the extent of democracy round the world. As per its analysis just 30 countries (comprising 14.4% of the world population) can be termed full democracies. Thus even though 80% of the world claims to have their own brand of democracy, in its true spirit, only about 14% of the world experiences a genuine democracy.

Measurement of economic freedom is far more robust and clear cut. The Index of Economic Freedom created by The Heritage Foundation and The Wall Street Journal rates nations on degree of economic freedom. Nations are measured on 10 factors like monetary freedom, labor freedom, lack of corruption etc. which are then used to derive the composite index. The Heritage foundation reports that the top 20% index nations have twice the per capita income of those in the second quintile and five times those of the bottom 20%. Unable to provide a similar justification for its index, the Freedom house is quick to claim that there is high degree of correlation between its freedom index and economic freedom index. Even a quick comparison of the two indices points out the incongruity. The top two ranks of economic freedom are occupied by Hong Kong and Singapore. Both are rated partly free in the Freedom index with Singapore close to bottom range of that. It seems our understanding of what works in economics has evolved better than in politics.

Another important index is the "Press Freedom Index" compiled by Reporters without Borders. It is based on a survey of correspondents, journalists and activists round the world and measures direct and indirect pressures on press. The top ranks are dominated by the developed world and most of them seem to enjoy great press freedom as is well known. Surprisingly, the African nations do fairly well on press freedom index[1] as compared to developing countries in other regions. Even with all their problems, at least there is greater transparency, which is commendable.

If we were to truly measure degree of freedom in the world as per the three freedom needs identified, we may focus on different kind of indices. The first measure of physical freedom would denote the right to exist without harm or violence in daily life. Crime statistics per se are an unreliable source as they seem highest in the most lawful of nations where people take the trouble to report or record a crime. The "Global Peace Index" would be a good starting measure as to the degree of physical freedom as it measures crime and threat from other citizens as a part of the index. But it has a skew on military expenditures which absolves smaller countries that depend on larger ones to protect them, as noted by the *Economist*. Travel books and travel companies and even government travel ministries document the level of crime in various nations to a good extent. Perhaps information compiled from these sources can be used to define basic physical freedom. Freedom from poverty is already a well-measured index with poverty statistics available across all countries along with their past trends. Likewise freedom of expression and political freedom are measured through the press freedom index and the democracy index. Different nations in different stages of economic and social development may focus on different aspects of freedom,

---

1 Press Freedom Index, 2002 — 2009, Wikipedia, the free encyclopedia, http://en.wikipedia.org/wiki/Press_Freedom_Index

most relevant to their citizens' needs. Overall a nation should be measured on all three aspects of freedom to see where it stands, on a stand-alone basis, vis-à-vis others, and also in regard to the direction in which it is moving.

To sum up, freedom is an important goal for mankind and it is within our reach. To achieve it, we must be clear in our definition, making sure what we call "freedom" is relevant to people living vastly different realities in different parts of the world. Freedom of expression is a higher order need that has been a catalyst in human advancement. Yet, in the absence of the first two basic needs of physical and economic freedom, freedom of speech becomes a mere pacifier. Democracy has been superior to any other system in propagating freedom of expression. But its ability to deliver on the two basic freedom dimensions is in doubt in the developing world. Thus once again transient political models need to be evolved for the developing world such that they meet human kind's most basic freedom needs first. However, once a nation has developed, democracy is the only known political model which completes the freedom pyramid.

CHAPTER 9. THE VERDICT: DEVELOPMENT OR DEMOCRACY?

To sum up, there is a widening gap between democracy as a theory and as a society form in practice. If democracy is not an end in itself but a means to good governance, it has not done too well. While supposedly a solution to the problems of the developing world, in practice democracy has more often led to instability, civil wars, genocides, fundamentalism, crime and corruption. Countless nations have been torn apart in the aftermath of a political opening up—Congo, Kenya, Nigeria, Pakistan, Indonesia, Iraq; the list is long. Even in India, the most celebrated example of a democracy in the developing world, divisions along caste, religion and language lines permeate the entire social fabric.

In these opportunity-starved nations, a seat in the parliament is a quick and easy road to riches and power. Criminals and local warlords often tend to join politics at the grassroots, relying on divisive tactics to develop vote banks and electoral violence is second nature to these demagogues. Parties rely more on freebies and divisive tactics to win elections since these have instant appeal, especially to poor voters who view long term development programs with suspicion, assuming they will never see the benefit. This does not somehow magically add up to good governance. The decaying state of filth and misery is all too apparent upon a visit to any of these nations.

Yet we are neither able nor willing to reconcile the difference between this "reality" and our theories. At the heart of our denial is our inability to see a progressive alternative and a fear that the mere process of challenging democracy will take us back to tyrannies whereas it is not challenging that will, or has already. We tend to rationalize its repeated failures, and blame it on the respective countries' politicians, bureaucrats, corporations; but democracy always gets away. It is time to come clean and acknowledge democracy's failure in the developing world and start focusing on finding political solutions that actually work in reality.

Democracy holds a strong appeal because of its apparent success in the developed world. Prosperity, freedom and respect for human rights are powerful allures for rest of the world, and they tend to go hand in hand with democracy. But if there is a causal relationship, which way does it run? As experience teaches, the end result cannot just be copied; there is a process to get there. The developed nations too were polarized societies with landed aristocracy at the top and a vast poor multitude at the bottom, two to three centuries back. As they moved to parliamentary governments, voting rights remained limited and were only gradually extended to the entire population, going in tandem with economic empowerment. This enabled stability through the birth pangs of industrialization and development. The prosperous, educated and hopeful middle class that arose as a result of this development handled power differently from the largely poor and rural majorities in the developing world. Also, the centuries leading up to democratization in Europe were marked by great social and intellectual advancement in the form of the Renaissance, the Scientific Revolution and the Age of Enlightenment. These helped pave the way for political openness.

Democracy, thus, is not a ready-to-install product but a process. A nation has to undergo evolution socially as well as economically before it is ready to take on the mantle of people power. In our eagerness to have the fruit of liberty, we want to skip all the painstaking stages of its formation and demand that a seed turn into a fruit on command. If it were so simple, every nation could somehow be made to write a constitution, hold free elections and bingo, all the problems of the poor countries would be solved. But in reality when we jump gun like this, we not only fail to solve the existing problems of poverty but to our horror we often let loose bigger catastrophes. While democracy is a worthy end goal, there is a crying need for a transient political model to help put these struggling developing nations on a progressive path. What might those transient models look like?

BEGINNING WITH THE END—GOVERNANCE GOALS

In order to work out the transient model/s for the developing world, it is imperative to understand what end we are seeking. Whether we acknowledge it or not, for quite some time now, democracy has been an end in itself. That is the foremost criterion on which all nations have been assessed and also the direction in which they have been pushed. The underlying assumption or suggestion is that democracy automatically leads to good governance, respect for human rights, and development. Based on a vast amount of evidence over the last 60 years, democracy has destabilized most developing nations and in the process sabotaged itself. For nation after nation, this "end" that we have chased has turned out to be a mirage. In the first place, for any nation, democracy should always be defined as a "means," never the "end." Good governance should be the appropriate "end," definable in terms of different goals for different nations based on their local socioeconomic context.

Democracy as a model has its limitations. While it might be the right system for pursuing higher order goals, it may be and has been totally inadequate and counterproductive in pursuing certain other, more basic goals. For instance, in nations like DR Congo and Afghanistan, the right goals should be ending the wars and insurgencies and establishing some form of law and order on the ground. With these objectives in mind, the leaders need to roll up their sleeves and take charge of their army or troops, not sit in a parliament and preside over debates on the finer nuances of laws which have not one iota of meaning outside the four walls of the assembly. Once basic political stability is achieved, economic activity can be encouraged.

Freedom of expression and participative governance would remain elusive goals for these kinds of fragile nations for some time to come. Since time immemorial, emergency measures have been used during periods of instability. But today, we have instead defined democracy as the instant and end goal and all of these fragile nations are pursuing it with disastrous results. Democracy is absolutely the wrong model in this kind of a scenario. We discuss this in greater detail under each category. Presently, it suffices to recognize that a separate set of goals need to be established for developing nations which sit on vastly different points of the socioeconomic development curve. These can be divided into three broad categories—war-torn nations, developing nations which already have some form of democracy, and those that do not.

As per the United Nations, good governance has eight major characteristics: participation, rule of law, transparency, responsiveness, consensus orientation, equity and inclusiveness, effectiveness & efficiency, and accountability. These goals might be highly appropriate for the developed nations but are pie in the sky for the developing ones. Given the complexity of our world and the vastly different realities people are living on this very planet, we need more sophisticated political thinking that takes these complexities into account rather than one objective and one solution—both apparently democracy—fits all. It just seems bringing in democracy and establishing it is hard work, real hard work but one that does not yield much returns to the nations or its peoples. Might not it be better to yield to easier options that enjoy higher returns?

DEVELOPMENT GOALS—DOING IT THE HARD WAY

While differentiated objectives for different sets of nations are warranted, economic development is a common goal for all these nations. Human Development Index[1] or the HDI and population below poverty line are two estimates that determine how a nation is doing in reality. HDI combines three dimensions—Life expectancy, education and per capita GDP. Before crafting a way forward, let us look at a snapshot of some of these nations.

Of all the African nations, Ghana is regarded as the most democratic one. It has a stable multiparty democracy with free elections and an administration considered hard working and relatively corruption free. Yet its HDI is only 0.526, barely above the 0.5 cut off for least developed economies. What is more worrying is that this index has been falling since 2000, when it was 0.568 which dropped to 0.553 in 2005 and now even lower. About 30% of its population is purported to be below poverty line. So where is democracy taking Ghana? Nigeria, which has struggled hard to establish democracy amidst ethno-religious differences, has achieved an HDI of just 0.511. Alarmingly, 64.4% of its population is below the poverty line despite being an oil rich nation. In Africa, the non democratic nations have been more stable as well as relatively more prosperous. Libya has achieved a high index of 0.847,

---

1 HDI — Human development Index 1975 — 2005, United Nations Development Program (UNDP), The World Factbook, http://www.photius.com/rankings/ human_developement_index_1975-2005.html

Egypt 0.703 and Algeria 0.754. Further, the population below the poverty line is less than 10% in any of these nations. South Africa inherited an HDI of 0.745 in 1995. With establishment of constitutional democracy and free elections, its HDI steadily slipped to 0.707 in 2000 to 0.674 in 2005 and now marginally better at 0.683 in 2007.

So essentially, many of these nations are not developing but actually receding. That is worrisome as many of them have worked hard to reach the present state of government.

Coming to India, the most celebrated developing world democracy in the world. With diversity like none other, it has taken India tremendous initiative and hard work to make democracy work. Before its economic reforms India had an HDI of just 0.521 in 1990 which has gone up to 0.612 now. It is better than many of the African nations but still ranked 134th in the world. The index has also stagnated over the last few years; in fact it was marginally better at 0.619 in 2005. 41.6% of its population remains below poverty line and roughly the same is illiterate as well. India has made a success of "the end in itself," democracy but that has not made a success of the nation. The inevitable comparison with China is increasingly obsolete as the latter with an HDI of 0.772 and 15.9% population below poverty line is no more the right benchmark for India.

It seems establishing a democracy and making it work is real hard work and creditworthy are the developing nations that have undertaken this Herculean task. But where are the returns? It is always important therefore to not confuse means with the ends. The ends should be development goals measurable in terms of poverty alleviation and HDI, the latter in turn incorporates parameters on education, health and prosperity. Democracy was, is and always should be a means to these ends. It is a way of forming the government. Lot more importance should be given to what the government achieves when in the seat of power than how it got there. Believing that a majority rule automatically leads to development and progressive ideals has been discredited amply by the developing world. Might not it be better to give a chance to the "far easier" governance models and see where they take development?

WAR-TORN NATIONS—EMERGENCY CALL

Throughout history, war times have necessitated emergency measures to re-establish control. These have never been the best of times for a society to undergo political renaissance. Yet that is what we have been attempting in Congo, Afghanistan, etc., predictably with dismal results.

The history of nations like the UK show that when they were undergoing civil wars, their intellectuals too propounded and supported the idea of a central authority needing to take control even at the expense of suspending some civil liberties. During the English civil war (1642–1651), Thomas Hobbes wrote a landmark book, *Leviathan*[1], which was published in 1651. He described the civil war as a "war of all against all"—*bellum omnium contra omnes*, leading to lives that are "solitary, poor, nasty, brutish, and short." He argued for a social contract with an absolute sovereign who rules with authority. He believed that chaos or civil wars could only be averted by a strong central government. To escape this state of war, a civil society would need a sovereign authority to whom all individuals in that society cede their natural rights for the sake of protection. He even went so far as to say that any abuses of power by this authority are to be accepted as the price of peace, although in severe cases of abuse, rebellion is expected and would be the corrective mechanism. Instead of being ridiculed, *Leviathan* became an important piece of work that established the foundation for the social contract theory, an important tenet of Western political philosophy. The book's perspective was understood at the time, as the political intellectuals lived in war times themselves. While there also were philosophers writing opinions to the contrary, many thinkers of the era advocated strengthening the authority and believed that any open kind of political systems could only exacerbate anarchy.

Fast forward to our times. Nations like Democratic Republic of Congo, Afghanistan, Iraq and to a lesser extent even Pakistan are undergoing insurgency and violence on a scale that could aptly be described as "war of all against all." A clear turn away from democracy and a turn to strong centralized governments will likely stabilize most of these nations.

---

1 Leviathan by Thomas Hobbes, Chapter 13-14, ebooks@Adelaid 2007, http://ebooks.adelaide.edu.au/h/hobbes/thomas/h68l/

The Democratic "Ruined" Republic of Congo

The number of casualties in the Congo civil war is estimated to be over 5 million. To get an idea of the catastrophic size of this war, this is greater than the whole population of Darfur or Palestine. Further, the toll is mounting at the last estimated rate of 45,000 per month. Apart from that, millions of refugees and internally displaced people have been created. Congo is a vast country, almost the size of Western Europe. The worst affected Eastern bordering region is thousands of miles from the capital Kinshasa in the Western most region of Congo. The war ruined East lacks any access to basic amenities like water, electricity, roads, jails, schools, hospitals etc. as whatever little infrastructure existed earlier has got destroyed in the war. Heinous brutalities have been unleashed against women and children in the region—by rebel militias, government troops as well as common men. It is one of the worst, if not the worst ever, civil wars in the history of mankind. What is the real problem and what could be the possible ways of stopping this?

As a starting premise, anytime, a war goes on too long, we can close our eyes and pin the tail. It is always the "local leadership" that is too weak. To briefly recap, this kind of violence is not a cultural problem in DR Congo. It was a peaceful state first as a Belgian colony and then under Mobutu Sese Seko's thirty-year-long stable authoritarian rule. He was overthrown by rebel leader Laurent-Désiré Kabila in 1997, ostensibly to establish democracy, but that did not happen. A civil war started as various rebel factions wrestled for control. The Eastern bordering region where refugees had spilled over from Rwandan genocide in 1994 was the starting base for all of these rebels who used ethnic factionalism and violence to build their loyalty bases. Bordering Rwanda and Uganda, too, were involved in the conflict. Post Kabila's assassination in 2001, his son Joseph Kabila became the president of the nation. While he signed a lot of paper deals, the war continued unabated. In 2006, democracy was established and Kabila won the elections on account of his slain father's ethnic following in the East.

The war deteriorated in 2008 and violence started spreading to other regions as well. Some International leaders have visited the region and the war has been covered occasionally in media as well. But no clear way forward seems in sight other than doing more of the same[1]. Further, despite the war escalating to hideous levels in the last decade when the same leader has been in power, there is no international condemnation of the leadership or pressure to resign on moral grounds as would have happened if he was a dictator. The underlying message is governance is only expected of dictators, for democratic leaders the only objective is winning elections not delivering any form of governance. So long as they can do that and do pretty much nothing else, they continue to enjoy international support.

In 2010, as if almost undaunted by rising chaos and indifferent to the humanitarian crisis, Kabila kicked off his 2011 election campaign with Golden jubilee celebrations in the capital Kinshasa, attended by dignitaries like the UN secretary Ban Ki Moon[2]. In the meantime Kabila's key political opponents, Nkunda and Bemba, have been indicted in war crimes as troops under them had committed atrocities during the war. By the same logic government troops presumably under President Kabila have committed greater atrocities, yet he can continue in power as he is "elected" and seemingly engages in good PR with the International visitors. It might have been better for the people of Congo if they had a dictator in power. Firstly, the law and order might have been better, second, at least their crisis would have been highlighted in the world in the required earnestness. Instead of Golden jubilee celebrations, the nation ought to be in mourning and should declare a state of emergency. UN too should perhaps declare a day of mourning for the victims of DR Congo War. To forge its way forward, Congo can look at the model in the neighboring Rwanda, which has successfully ended a deadly civil war and re-established order. DR Congo's solution lies in re-establishing a strong rule under a unitary system with a clear one line objective of controlling the war in reality. The current leadership can be given a year to prove its mettle and if not should be pressurized to resign on moral grounds. However, the likely next leadership may come from existing erstwhile rebel leaders. It is a fact that troops under all leaders, including the incumbent president, have committed crimes against civilians. The ensuing leadership cannot have "no past" and will have to be one of the existing rebel

1 DRC Politics, The Politics of Continuity? Hans Hoebeke, Feb/Mar 2010, african. org, http://www.egmontinstitute.be/papers/10/afr/100201-Hoebeke-politics-of-continuity-DRC.html

2 UN Chief Attends DR Congo's Golden Jubilee Celebrations, 25 Jun 2010, Afrique Avenir, http://www.afriqueavenir.org/en/2010/06/25/un-chief-attends-dr-congo%E2%80%99s-golden-jubilee-celebrations/

leaders unless a leader is chosen by lucky draw from the common populace as was sometimes done in ancient Greece under direct democracy to elect certain officials. All the existing leaders, one of whom at least is capable of controlling this war, will come with baggage; that is the inconvenient truth. So, like in Rwanda, a process of forgiveness and moving forward may have to be instituted. The path to ending war and reconstruction should follow the Rwandan model. A strong leader needs to takes charge of his troops and control them first as they are the biggest criminals in the present scenario. Once violence is brought under control, a strong one party rule could be established. DR Congo could bounce back better as it is a resource rich state but at present these resources are being deployed by the rebels in the opaque market to fund the war.

Iraq—Destiny Slipping, Yet Again

After years of chaos, Iraq showed signs of improvement about mid 2009, when Iraqi security forces as well as local leadership stepped up and took active charge[1]. But post the March 2010 elections, it is slipping back to where it started. Let us briefly review. Post Saddam's overthrow, an Iraqi transitional government was established under Ayad Allawi. He was a secularist and proved to be a strong leader. Despite belonging to the majority Shia community, he gained tremendous popularity with the minority Sunnis. In 2005, however, democracy was established and sectarian parties won their respective vote blocs. Quite naturally, then, Nouri-al Maliki, belonging to the dominant Shia alliance, became Prime Minister with Jalal Talabani of the third group, the Kurds, as President. The sectarian battles worsened and Iraq came close to a civil war in 2006–2007. The terrorist networks had largely been absent under Saddam's harsh regime which was intolerant of insurgency. Post 2003, al Qaeda had also made inroads into Iraq and a militant wing was also formed under al Sadr to end the US occupation. Anarchy and violence went up considerably.

But slowly, al-Maliki wrested control of the nation and brought down the violence. Iraqi forces took charge of the nation's security and a civil war was averted. As violence always turns inwards, crime went up in Iraq as the disbanded militants now harassed civilian Iraqis through kidnappings

---

1 "Maliki Says Iraq Needs Him as Leader," Anthony Shadid, 9 Jun 2010, *The New York Times*, http://www.nytimes.com/2010/06/10/world/middleeast/10maliki.html

and extortion[1]. But the political leadership in Iraq was turning more moderate. Al-Maliki, earlier considered divisive, also slowly moved away from the original Shia Alliance and formed a more moderate wing. At the same time, Grand Ayatollah Sayyed Ali al-Sistani, who has always stood against violence, also stated that he preferred not to have religion involved in the political process. In the 2010 election, Ayad Allawi and al-Maliki garnered the most votes but were roughly equal at about 24–25% each. The third largest winner was the Shia Alliance backed by al Sadr, whose militant movement was opposed by both Allawi and al Maliki. For either leader to become PM he would have to form a coalition with al Sadr. Yet coalition talks between such arch rivals broke down. Even 5–6 months after the elections, no potential coalition government seemed in sight.

Just when Iraq was stabilizing and its leadership was moving to the center-moderate position, once again democracy has altered the game. The power vacuum at the top is an open invitation for divisive forces and this could potentially turn the clock back. Instead of pulling out, US troops may have to be added back.

But, on the brighter side, Iraq has not one but two leaders, Allawi and Maliki, with proven administrative credentials. As a likely way forward, they could possibly rescue their nation by forming a unity government. This would be somewhat like the National Front formed in Colombia in 1957 post the decade-long bloodshed called *La Violencia*. The national government where the two large parties compromised and joined hands, helped end the large scale violence and put Colombia back on the path to progress. The model could be studied for its seeming fit with Iraq's current impasse. But this solution is only a theoretical ideal as indeed negotiations between Maliki and Allawi have not fructified. While the modalities of the leadership remain dependent upon local negotiations, the point remains that Iraq needs a strong centralized government under a central command structure to pull it out of this crisis. A fractious and destabilizing democracy will keep it mired in factional infighting and violence. Stability in Iraq long term depends upon the ability of the local leadership to take charge. But a centrally-controlled empowered form of government may be necessary as opposed to a diffused, weak and even divisive democratic form. This may be an important consideration against our present erroneous political as-

---

1   After Years of War, Iraqis Hit by Frenzy of Crime, 21 Spt 2009, Associated Press, msnbc.com, http://www.msnbc.msn.com/id/32955876/

sumptions for nations in a state of war, where we believe democracy is the right model.

Afghanistan and Pakistan

The war on terror is a far more complex war with many underlying reasons and influences. It is also a costly war where an estimated $300 billion[1] has already been sunk and the costs are further escalating every year. According to former Saudi intelligence chief Turki al-Faisal, what Afghanistan needs is a shift from supposed nation building to effectively countering terrorists[2]. He believes that the "US should not be misdirected into believing that they can fix Afghanistan's ills." According to him, the forces should just focus on tackling terrorists on both sides of the Afghan–Pakistan border. Let us see some part of wisdom in his words. Afghanistan is a nation in ruins with an HDI of 0.352, almost the lowest in the world. Apart from destitution and lack of order, the nation is riven by a multitude of now fiercely hostile ethnic and linguistic groups. Given these conditions, this is absolutely the last place to establish democracy. That is perhaps what al-Faisal means when he suggests that occupying forces should abandon the nation-building goals and instead focus on just the terror network. This was the original aim of the war, but it was never achieved as the occupying forces got distracted into chasing the ever elusive mirage of democracy. Perhaps a turn away from democracy to a centralized command and strong rule of local leadership in Afghanistan as well as Pakistan, among other measures, may help end this war. How soon the problems are tackled still depends upon the quality and strength of the local leadership that emerges in each of these nations. But there already is a complete breakdown of authority and structure in these societies and pursuit of an open system like democracy would only weaken it further and also lead decentralized power back into the hands of the insurgents.

Some international experts have also suggested that Afghans need jobs to overcome the insurgency. That is putting the cart before the horse. Unless there is at least a modicum of peace and stability, no economic activity is

---

1 The Cost of Iraq, Afghanistan and Other Global War on Terror Operations Since 9/11, Amy Belasco, 28 Sept 2009, Congressional research Service, http://www.fas. org/sgp/crs/natsec/RL33110.pdf

2 Inept US Cannot Fix Afghanistan : Top Saudi Prince, 16 May 2010, The Times of India, http://timesofindia.indiatimes.com/world/middle-east/Inept-US-cannot-fix-Afghanistan-Top-Saudi-prince/articleshow/5935808.cms

viable. Economic revival no doubt should be a part of the long term solution to the problem but in the current circumstances of widespread violence and a "war of all against all," no industry can survive. A strong centralized rule has to be established first that controls violence and establishes some form of law and order before even rudimentary economic activity is possible.

In Pakistan too violence has worsened since 2008—since the fall of Musharraf's regime and the reinstating of democracy. The Taliban has gained strength in Pakistan, which perhaps is a contributor to its becoming stronger than before in Afghanistan too. By early 2009, Tehreek-e-Taliban Pakistan (TTP) had recreated fiefdoms in the Swat Valley and tribal areas of North West Pakistan. This was quelled by another military operation by the new government, although it only managed to disperse the groups not destroy them. These groups have staged terror attacks throughout Pakistan. Further, in many provinces like Punjab, several of the earlier banned militant groups have now become elected representatives[1]. US military aid to combat terrorism has also gone up substantially. Earlier, when a strong regime was in power, the US was spending an average of $ 600 million per annum in Pakistan; this went up to $1.5 billion per annum post 2009. In addition, a further sum of $ 2.8 billion was pledged, given the gains Taliban had made under the fractious weak and ineffective quasi democracy now in place on both sides of the border.

Furthermore if democracy is the answer to everything, how come armies are top-down hierarchical organizations? Imagine how they would fight wars if they were turned into democratic forms and were expected to call an assembly which could deliberate on the finer nuances of each decision. That is what is being attempted in these regions or nations that are engaged in a "war of all against all." War time requires a strong centralized hierarchical control structure with clear lines of command. Once the war ends and peace is attained in a sustainable manner, systems become important too, but to pull out of war requires power vested in strong central leadership.

Democracy is a poor system when the majority of the populace is unprepared for it, and the situation is made even worse when the nation is also in a state of war. Then it is part of the problem, not the solution. To go back to the starting premise, wars require emergency measures, not politi-

---

1 Pakistan Attacks Point to Resurgent Extremism, Saeed Shah, 6 Apr 2010, Global Post, http://www.globalpost.com/dispatch/pakistan/100406/pakistan-suicide-bombings-funerals-consulate?page=0,1

cal renaissance or opening up. In the state of *bellum omnium contra omnes*, as propounded by Thomas Hobbes' theory of social contract, a civil society can be established through a sovereign authority to whom all individuals in that society cede their natural rights for the sake of protection. That perhaps is the way forward for the war torn regions of Congo, Iraq, Afghanistan, Pakistan, etc. Under strong leaders in an empowered centralized government format, the nations still have a chance to be rescued. How soon or effectively these wars can be controlled however depends greatly on the nature of the local leadership that emerges in these nations. In Rwanda, Paul Kagame proved to be a powerful leader and was instrumental in controlling the civil war. The Congo war has gone on longer, in a bigger region, and is harder to resolve. But a strong leader who could control the troops would help arrest the war. In other regions too, the emergence of strong local leadership in an empowered centralized rule format would provide the key to bringing down violence in many of these war torn nations.

THE MISUNDERSTOOD EXILES

Myanmar

In the world of free markets, free trade and globalization, very few nations face international sanctions today. In the past South Africa's apartheid regime was one such example. In recent times, along with nations like Zimbabwe and Iran there is a far lesser known country on whom international sanctions have been imposed, Myanmar, earlier called Burma. What has it done to earn this status?

Myanmar, a diverse society with multiple ethnic groups, had a long stint with democracy post independence in 1948 till 1962. This led to a series of political and ethnic insurrections as well as assassinations inspired by political rivalry. Communal secessionist movements started in all its bordering regions, some spilling over to neighboring India and Thailand as well. Myanmar's democratic government was largely ineffective in dealing with this rising militancy. Further, in the 1960s, U Nu, the incumbent leader, wished to install Buddhism as the state religion since his religious credentials had helped him win the elections. Dissatisfied with the deteriorating law and order and now the turn to religion, the secularist military toppled this regime. Since then it has shared an uneasy relationship with the monks and religious society. Under this regime, Myanmar was tightly controlled and the economy turned socialist, with nationalization of industries, as was indeed done in most developing countries at the time. By late 1980s Myanmar started feeling the need for a change. The economy had slowed down, student protests were common and Aung San Suu Kyi, the slain leader's daughter, returned and led the democracy movement. Under mounting pressure, the army finally agreed to hold elections in 1989. Initial results indicated a landslide victory for Suu Kyi's NLD party, thus ruling out a joint parliament that the military regime was hoping for. Further, NLD leaders started talking about a "Nürnberg style" trial of the military leaders in power. This was perhaps politically motivated, as most NLD members were and still are ex military themselves. Threatened by these developments, the military regime backtracked on its tentative march towards democracy. But post 1990s, as erstwhile UN officer and historian Thant Myint-U points out,[1] the military regime underwent a drastic change. While politics remained centralized, the new leadership started liberalizing the economy.

As before, Myanmar continued following a harmonious and responsible foreign policy and maintained friendly relations with all its neighbors. Insurgencies along the Chinese and the Indian borders were controlled, and that helped stabilize the region. Drugs production and mafias were systematically routed from the golden drug triangle by cooperation between Myanmar, China and Thailand. Suu Kyi's family members were allowed to visit her and her detention was also relaxed. Most separatist movements were dealt with through military force earlier. Now the government negotiated with guerrillas and struck deals for ceasefire. By the mid 1990s Myanmar had successfully negotiated calm and peace within its borders. A militant community of Karens still held out but they have been kept under check (else they may have turned into a wing like the LTTE in Sri Lanka). But since the 1990s when the Myanmar leadership transformed, the nation started facing crippling international sanctions. The regime is rightly criticized for its autocratic tendencies and endless military rule is certainly the wrong system for any nation. However, there are some softer aspects of the military regime's governance that also need to be highlighted. As per the 1953–54 census, illiteracy in Myanmar stood at 36.2 %. A literacy drive[2] was

---

1 What to do About Burma, Thant Myint-U, 8 Feb 2007, LRB Vol 29, http://www. lrb.co.uk/v29/n03/-thantmyint-u/what-to-do-about-burma

2 Development of Education in Burma 1975-76, Ministry of Education, 36th Session of the International Conference on Education, Geneva, 1977, UNESCO, http://

launched between 1966 and 1974 whereby a village by village and district by district comprehensive systematic literacy operation was carried out. In 1971 the government received recognition from UNESCO for its work in the literacy field.

UNICEF provides some comparative statistics. Myanmar's literacy rate today is 90%, just slightly behind China's 93%. The comparative figures for democratic countries are India 66%, Ghana 65% and Pakistan 55%. Myanmar also made concerted efforts in providing basic health care, despite its limited resources. In terms of malnutrition statistics, infants with low birth weight are 15% for Myanmar, well above China's 4% and even Ghana's 9% but lower than India's 28% or Pakistan's 32%. In terms of improved sanitation facilities, one of the key hygiene factors in the developing world, Myanmar has achieved a rate of 82% of the population, well ahead of even China at 65% and certainly others like India at 28%, Pakistan 58% and Ghana 36%. Since water communicable diseases like diarrhea are common, medical care like re-hydration and continued feeding are critical to save lives. Children under 5 who received such care is 65% in Myanmar, 29% Ghana, 33% India and 37% Pakistan. China has a negligible incidence of such problems now. All the above progress has been made despite the lack of any outside assistance. Myanmar continues to face oppressive sanctions from the West. Despite that, it has managed to score an HDI of 0.586, higher than Ghana at 0.526 or Pakistan at 0.572 and only a little behind India's 0.612. This has mainly been on account of good performance on education and health parameters though its per capita income remains low due to its isolation.

So Myanmar is under crippling international sanctions because it does not have democracy? As Thant Myint U points out, the military is the only institution in the nation. If it is summarily dismantled, the country will be destabilized, given its ethnic divides.[1] It has active to semi-active secessionist movements amongst the Arakan, Chin, Kachin, Karen, Karenni, Kuki, Shan, Wa and a few others. Most of these have been kept under check, as in Indonesia under Sukarno. A violent overthrow of the existing power structure and forceful establishment of democracy in all likelihood will destabilize this nation. Given its diversity and its legacy of insurgency, militancy as well as the drugs trade will also likely get a fresh breath of life. Alternative-

---

www.ibe.unesco.org/National_Reports/Myanmar/nr_mf_br_1977_e.pdf

1 Missing the Point on Myanmar, Charles McDermid, in conversation with Thant Myint-U, 4 Jul 2009, Asia Times online, http://www.atimes.com/atimes/Southeast_Asia/KG04Ae01.html

ly, Myanmar could try for a peaceful transition to a single party rule where power is shared by the military and representatives from the NLD. There should be a fixed term rotation of the top leadership, but ideally, Aung San Suu Kyi should be its rightful first leader. She could add tremendous value in reintegrating the nation with the rest of the world. But the transition to a more open system has to involve the current regime, not initiate trials against them. It is important to recognize the existing power structure in a nation and to not underestimate the importance of stability and order, nor take them for granted. A quick change to democracy, brought about by intense external international pressure, will not turn Myanmar into a US, UK or a Germany. It will become a part of the troubled Asian region with escalating violence like Indonesia, Thailand, and Pakistan.

If Myanmar were to look for role models in the region, it should look at successful governments that have achieved good progress under ethnically diverse circumstances, like Singapore or even the emergent Vietnam.

Vietnam—Truth is Mightier than the Sword

A costly war was fought by the US to contain "communism" (that is, pro-Chinese or pro-Soviet factions) in Vietnam during the Cold War era. The withdrawal of US forces followed by the capture of Saigon by the North Vietnamese army in 1975 marks the end of this long war. Thus the Communists remained unbeaten and thereafter followed their earlier policies even more staunchly. North and South Vietnam were unified, all farms were collectivized and the economy remained under tight state controls. However, even a decade later, the economy had not revived. Upset by this lack of progress, reformers emerged from within the system. In 1986, the party leadership underwent a complete makeover and the old guard was replaced with new leaders. The nation started changing its economic policies. Ironically, having resisted capitalism in a war of nearly two decades, the Communist Party of Vietnam (VCP) now voluntarily adopted the very policies it had fought against. It started implementing free market reforms in what is known as the Doi Moi revolution. Like China, the political authority remained centralized but the economy was opened up in a carefully managed transition. Farms and industries were privatized, markets were deregulated and foreign investment encouraged. This is what the entire war was fought over yet had failed to achieve. Now Vietnam had done it voluntarily, with the VCP realizing the need for economic liberalization and foreign investment, on its own. While Vietnam was no model of democracy, it achieved a consistent 7–8% GDP growth since 1990, making it the second fastest growing economy in the world. It is also considered one of Asia's most open economies—two-way trade is around 160% of GDP, more than twice the ratio for China and over four times the same for India. Its Human Development Index today is 0.725, almost midway between India's 0.612 and China's 0.772. Centralized politics and a decentralized economy seem to have worked in many of these largely poor nations.

DETERIORATING YET COMPLACENT—MOST DEVELOPING WORLD DEMOCRACIES

Many nations have established some form of democracy but are on a destructive, declining path of alarming violence, corruption and anarchy. These are majority of democratic nations in the developing world like Nigeria, South Africa, Kenya, Bangladesh, and Indonesia. A lot of them are called failed states and often there is a feeling of hopelessness about them as well. Yet what are the solutions offered to them? So far, there has been just "democracy". Many of these states have undergone political opening up and a great amount of effort has been put into drafting constitutions, creating electoral systems and also in finally conducting elections, holding assemblies, etc. Yet things have deteriorated. It can't be the fault of democracy *per se*, as it does work rather well in the developed world. So it is "them"; the people just don't understand democracy well enough. So now, nothing can be done except keep trying harder.

But look at our own conclusion: "people do not understand democracy." If they do not understand, it means they aren't ready for it, not yet. Democracy works in the developed world because they have a substantial middle class, and the working poor identify with the middle class. Hypothetically, if the poor people that unfortunately do still exist in the developed nations were able to come together and act as a majority there, the resultant democracy would be very different from what it is today. The poor in the developing world are infinitely worse off than the derelicts of the developed world. That is why democracy is unstable as well as destabilizing in the developing world. If it is taking too much effort to establish, that is the first indicator that this is the wrong system for the society. Even after a concerted pursuit for over 50 years, only about 14% of the world's population experiences genuine democracy—as per the Democracy Index. So, there is a reason why it has not stabilized, and that reason is not lack of effort or will. In several nations, during the process of democratization, the national circumstances deteriorated sharply. If similar but non-democratic nations seem to be doing better, then all these indicators point to democracy being not the right model—that is perhaps why it is unstable as well as destabilizing.

Democracy no doubt is a worthy end goal but for it to work, as said before, these nations have to come up to a certain level of social and economic development. Until then, "rule by majority" is only going to add to the problems. In light of this practical reality, let us craft a way forward. Let us start by looking at the example of two failed states, Nigeria and Cameroon, followed by a discussion of India, Russia and China, to see specifically what can be done in each case. In the end we may be able to put together our learning on a political way forward for the developing world.

Nigeria—The Borderline Nation

Nigeria has high levels of poverty, corruption, and communal violence as well as general crime. Most of the communal violence has been instigated by local political leaders. In the oil delta, kidnappings, extortion and murder have become commonplace because of the nexus between politicians, criminals and security forces at the local level. However, Nigeria has seen some stability since the return of its earlier military leader, Olusegun Obasanjo. In the late 1970s, he brought in constitutional changes to curb factionalism and regionalization of parties and voluntarily reinstated democracy. He decide to contest the 1999 election and won two successive terms post which he stepped down as per the two term limit. When he took over, Nigeria was particularly unstable, and as he himself said, "In 1999, Nigeria was not looking for a president that would build roads, fix power or provide water; Nigeria was looking for a president that would hold Nigerians together." Quite rightly then, he first focused on establishing stability in the volatile nation. Once that was achieved, the focus shifted to stimulating the economy, carrying out anti corruption drives and investing in infrastructure. The Nigerian economy started growing at about 6% p.a. In his tenure he was able to curb large scale riots but could not weed out violence as it is integrated with the democratic political structure[1]. In his earlier tenure as

---

1 Politicians are the Causes of Electoral Violence in Nigeria — APV, 13 Nov 2009, http://www.articlesbase.com/journalism-articles/politicians-are-the-causes-of-

a military head this kind of violence was remarkably absent or negligible. Since 2007 when he stepped down, he has continued to play an influential role which has helped Nigeria stay stable. Nigeria is better than it was a decade ago[1] but it still remains mired in large scale poverty and violence.

Nigeria is fortunate to have the right leader at hand who has proven his administrative abilities on the ground, but Nigeria is languishing under a system that cannot deliver much: democracy. A deliberate turn away from democracy is only scary to those who live in great prosperous countries. For people who live amidst violence, poverty and hopelessness, it would be a turn for the good. With concerted leadership, Nigeria has now inched up to an HDI of 0.511 whereas even a sleepy neighbor like Cameroon is 0.523. Let us look at Cameroon before exploring the way forward.

Cameroon—A Sleepy State

Let us see how doing nothing is better than doing the wrong thing. Cameroon is a nation adjoining Nigeria and has many similarities with the latter. It has over 250 different ethnic and linguistic groups and is also a multi religious society[2] with the presence of Christianity, indigenous religions and Islam. Like Nigeria, it is almost evenly divided between urban and rural. However that is where the similarities end. Cameroon has been a single party state since its independence in 1960. Since then, it has enjoyed high level of political and social stability; so much for the theory of tribalism in Africa being the reason behind its civil wars when indeed they have taken place mostly under democratic regimes. In 1990, Cameroon too was lured into introducing multi party democracy. Immediately it started to have regional splits and problems. Since colonial times, there have been English- and French-speaking areas in Cameroon. In 1990, Anglophone pressure groups called for greater autonomy with some advocating complete secession as the Republic of Ambazonia. This, along with a coup attempt, made

---

electoral-violence-in-nigeria-apv-1455350.html

1 Nigeria Needs Sustained Reforms to Build on Success, David Nellor, 15 Feb 2008, Annual IMF Economic Assessment, International Monetary Fund, http://www.imf.org/external/pubs/ft/survey/so/2008/CAR021508A.htm

2 Ethnicity, Violence and Multi-Party Democracy in Africa since 1989, Tata Simon Ngenge, University of Yaounde, Ethnonet Africa, Elicits how different tribal groups existed in Cameroon too. http://www.ethnonet-africa.org/pubs/p95ngenge.htm

the leader Paul Biya see the light and he has since staged elections to declare himself the winner.

Stability in Cameroon allowed for the development of agriculture, roads, railways and petroleum and timber industries but its economy remains rudimentary. The government has made some concerted efforts at containing corruption but, lacking in economic development, the task is difficult. It is a nation that could probably be a candidate for IMF assistance and reforms but since it does not have a democracy, it remains an outlier. With 32.8% of its population below the poverty line (half the rate in Nigeria), it is doing better than many African states. Cameroon is a laid back state but it has the same HDI as Ghana and slightly better than Nigeria. Maybe we have underestimated the importance of political stability.

As seen in Nigeria as well as briefly even in Cameroon and countless nations in the developing world, a turn to multi party democracy almost instantly leads to sectarian divides. This happens because at the grassroots, the local warlords and thugs take the easiest route to developing a vote bloc, through divisive means. Often ethnic groups that have coexisted peacefully for over centuries suddenly start clashing. That is why violent factionalism has risen in a chilling form in the post colonial world. Till there is violence, economic activity remains stunted.

In terms of a way forward, nations like Nigeria should consolidate state power. But instead of turning to military rule or cult dictatorships, they should aim for structured single party rule. In its present state, Nigeria may do well to start with its "proven" successful leader, Olusegun Obasanjo. His secular pan national leadership, administrative abilities and focus on the economy is what Nigeria needs. Democracy is the only obstacle that stands in the way. If that is cleared, the parliament can have representation from its diverse regional groups and perhaps allocate 30% seats to the women.

On the other hand, nations like Cameroon are never in the international limelight, ironically, because they are peaceful. Likewise, Tanzania too has been dominated by the CCM party since its independence in 1962. It has about 120 ethnic groups and also faced an influx of refugees from Rwanda–Burundi's infamous 1994 civil war. Refugees from Rwanda and Burundi had fled to DR Congo in the East and to Tanzania in the West. But the strong single party rule in the latter disallowed any spillover ethnic strife within its borders. In fact Tanzania often mediated to resolve the conflict in the region. Yet such nations are never in the news. Their stability and peace should be appreciated and not taken for granted. Perhaps if the present democracy-based apartheid is ended, such stable states can easily be made bustling centers of economic revival. But they lack the know-how which the IMF, World Bank etc. can easily provide. Why should failed states remain the poster child of Africa? Why not help liberalize the already peaceful and stable ones and give prosperity and human dignity a chance? International pressure groups may also help nations to focus on political stability and pressure them to invest in education and infrastructure and perhaps offer assistance in economic stimulation and opening up.

Kenya

In Kenya, the present coalition government between its two large parties already is a step in the proposed direction of a unity party rule. It seems to have worked in pulling the nation out of violence and chaos post the 2007 elections. However, contrary to what is being proposed here for the nation to consider, Kenya has passed a new constitution, approved in a referendum in August 2010, to decentralize power further—that by all logic thus far can only prove detrimental to its governance. Its problem of electoral violence is higher at the decentralized level. To curb that, it needs to centralize power like in the KANU era when the central government discouraged grassroots factionalism. Further, putting the constitutions up for referendum, as was done here, is an exercise that pleases the international media and opinion leaders but has little meaning in reality. With its elaborate legally worded clauses, this is a constitution that is hard to decipher for even a well aware, reasonably educated person. It is doubtful whether illiterate or barely literate people can understand and cast a genuine well considered vote on it. In all likelihood they just back their leaders who campaign for a yes or a no on the referendum, once again decided on the basis of personalities or ethnic alignments rather than what is actually written in the new constitution.

In India, for instance, it was realized early on that party names were sometimes confusing to the electorate and thus party symbols were invented, and most campaigns are built around these symbols. So even party names need symbols to communicate effectively with the voters; yet we believe they can somehow read and judge a long, elaborate and legally worded constitution. Well aware of this reality, India did not put its constitution up for a referendum; but this is increasingly done and encouraged as the right mechanism in most developing countries which too are dominated by the rural poor.

It may be helpful to validate some of our unrealistic belief in referenda and elections as they play out in reality. It may not be possible to transpose ideas from one part of the world to the next. What works in the developed world of "today" may not work in the developing one, given their vastly different realities.

India—The Looming Crisis

Post extensive legislative and executive efforts, India has now managed to have negligible electoral violence and rigging. Power changes hands peacefully and the national media is free. India is a pluralistic, tolerant society and minorities too enjoy significant rights, often holding even the highest offices, including those of the Prime Minister and President. The rule is as per the constitution and there is separation of powers among the judiciary, the executive and the legislative. The political leadership is largely tolerant of criticism and dissent and has tremendous ability to negotiate and compromise. India is also one of the first few nations to have electronic voting. So, this is a pretty good implementation of the processes of democracy. If democracy was an end in itself, India has made a reasonable success of it. But in more than 60 years of its earnest implementation, where has it taken the nation?

In terms of population, India at 1.2 billion and China at 1.3 billion individually are larger than the whole continents of Africa at just 922 million, Europe at 731 million or Latin America at 382 million. China's population growth rate has come down to 0.58%. India's is almost 2.5 times that and slightly higher than the world average. With 41.6% of India's population estimated to be below the poverty line and 34% also illiterate, the world's largest number of poor and illiterate live in India. Further development is restricted to the already overstretched metros and large towns and rural comprising 72% of the population. As per the World Bank, India is the largest user of ground water in the world which supports 60% of irrigated agriculture and 80% of water supplies. At the current rate of depletion, the water table is estimated to dry up in 15 years. This could potentially be India's first crisis call but despite warnings, no measures have been put into place. They are hard to implement as the leading cause of water depletion is wasteful agricultural practices in millions of small farms in the country.

Further, in terms of drinking water supply, most water sources are contaminated by sewage and agricultural runoffs. Lack of access to safe drinking water is a major source of communicable diseases, and diarrhea alone causes about 1600 deaths daily.[1]

India has a mechanistic federal structure that helped stabilize the nation through sharing of powers with its divergent states. But development is disparate with a laggard state like Bihar having a literacy rate of merely 47% and a per capita income of just $147,[2] which is comparable to some of the worst African countries. In fact the World Bank estimates acute poverty in 8 of the Indian states, similar to some of the poor ones in Africa. The disparity is reflected in people's attitudes as well. In a survey, 70% respondents considered loyalty to their region more important than loyalty to the nation; only 14% of respondents thought otherwise. Yet, India is a conciliatory and tolerant society, which has aided its stability.

While originally a part of the BRIC emerging economies bloc, it stands nowhere as compared to the others. In terms of HDI, Russia and Brazil have already crossed the threshold level of 0.8 for higher developed nations and China is closing in at 0.772, while India lags far behind at 0.612, alongside poor Asian and African nations. Its purchasing power parity income at $2,941 is less than half of China's at $6,567 and well behind Brazil and Russia at $10,514 and $14,920 respectively. There is a lot of euphoria around the GDP growth and India's presence in the knowledge economy, and those are clearly good signs to build on. But investment in education and infrastructure is inadequate. Government's drive to spread industrialization has been violently opposed. Democratic elections are primarily driven by distribution of freebies and divisive tactics based on caste, language, religion, etc. Crime is rising and women's status remains low with widespread oppressive practices like gender discrimination, the dowry system, and harassment. All of these problems are particularly bad in rural India where practices like female feticide and infanticide are also common in many of the backward states. The rural *dalits*, about 100–150 million people, remain among the most oppressed communities in the world. These are serious problems.

---

1 The Water and Sanitation Crisis, India, Water.org, http://water.org/projects/india/

2 Acute poverty in 8 Indian States, says New UNDP Measure, Prasun Sonwalkar, 12 Jul 2010, DNA India, http://www.dnaindia.com/india/report_acute-poverty-in-8-indian-states-says-new-undp-measure_1408795

Indian general elections continue to be an aggregate of 28 regional elections.[1] The two national parties, BJP and Congress, together accounted for just 47.36% of the votes in the 2009 national elections. The balance was won by regional parties that have mushroomed since the 1990s and rarely have any presence outside their respective states. As per the federal structure, the states already have their own elections and assemblies and enjoy tremendous powers. Through regionalization of the national vote, states have now indirectly usurped the national powers as well. India thus has a weak federal government which ends up operating in a coalition with divergent regional parties that have no common goals whatsoever. After a long time, the 2009 elections gave the Congress-led UPA a near majority but usually a split mandate is the norm.

India's only silver lining ironically is the national level leadership of its two parties, Congress and the BJP. Time and again they have followed conciliatory policies to maintain stability. When the BJP was in power it gave up its *Hindutva* agenda, seeing the riots, and turned to development as the goal and initiated dialogue with Pakistan to improve relations and resolve the issue of Kashmir. It did lose the election due to this, though. Likewise, Congress leadership put the SEZ drive on hold as it led to large scale violent protests among farmers and their opinion leaders. The national leadership has pursued harmonious and responsible foreign policies, often cooperating with neighbors and never inciting insurgency along their borders. They are largely tolerant of criticism and national level media has a lot of freedom though the same cannot be said of some of the state level governments. Since the 1990s, the leadership has undertaken market reforms and India has a robust private sector. While a naturally tolerant society, people have shown as much tendency to instigate violence as anywhere else in the poverty ridden world. The Gujarat riots bear testimony to that. However the divisive factors have not been played to a violent extent by the national politicians as they have been by some of the state level ones. BJP is still led by octogenarians who took part in the freedom struggle and Congress is led by the Nehru–Gandhi family with similar antecedents. These leaders have largely played a cohesive and progressive role but their base within is being eroded by regional divisive elements.

---

1 India's 2009 Elections : The Resilience of Regionalism and Ethnicity, Christophe Jaffrelot and Gilles Verniers, South Asia Multidisciplinary Academic Journal, SAMAJ, http://samaj.revues.org/index2787.html

India is hurtling towards a crisis. Its crisis calls may come from three different directions. One, as repeated alarms have warned, India's water table is fast depleting and this could present an emergency situation in 15 years' time.[1] Wasteful agricultural practices as well as an unabated population explosion are the key reasons for this. The shortage of water will threaten its availability for drinking as well as for agriculture, which will worsen the plight of the large farming community and create food shortages, especially in drought years. Two, India is a diverse nation and its democracy has over the last two decades been hijacked by divisive elements focused on caste, language and religion. This is gaining momentum day by day and could pose a risk to India's unity and stability. Last but not the least, its development agenda is based entirely on short term distribution of freebies; investment in infrastructure and education is lagging behind. This has already led India towards an inflationary economy to fund the huge budget deficits the government has been running. It is imperative to act now instead of waiting for these crises to disrupt the stable nation.

India's faults are not hidden as its crumbling state is more than obvious even to a casual visitor. Its key problem is its premature turn to universal suffrage democracy. There were many skeptics of mass democracy in the West about two centuries back when the Western world was also in a semi developed stage. Lord Macaulay, a British historian and politician born in 1800, criticized the democracy[2] of the time in his discussion with Henry Randall of New York. "Your constitution is all sail and no anchor. As I said before, when a society has entered this downward progress, either civilization or liberty must perish. I have long been convinced that institutions purely democratic must sooner or later, destroy liberty, or civilization, or both." He believed that unlike the earlier empires where the destroyers came from without, democracy's destroyers will come from within. This kind of skepticism kept the Western nations away from popular democracy when they too consisted predominantly of rural, poor classes. It is time to acknowledge that Indian democracy like many others in the developing

---

1 "India's Ground Water Table to Dry Up in 15 Years, World Bank calls for immediate corrective measures," Ajith Athrady, 7 Mar 2010, *Deccan Herald*, http://www.deccanherald.com/content/56673/indias-ground-water-table-dry.html

2 "Macaulay on Democracy: Curious Letter from Lord Macaulay on American Institutions and Prospects," 24 Mar 1860 The Southern Literary Messenger, *New York Times*, http://www.nytimes.com/1860/03/24/news/macaulay-democracy-curious-letter-lord-macaulay-american-institutions-prospects.html?pagewanted=1

world is all sail and no anchor. Despite India's creditworthy achievements of respecting civil liberties, freedom of expression and stable constitutional rule, democracy has failed to develop India in tune with its rising demands.

So far, the developing world has been replete with examples of failed states but in the last decade or two, several erstwhile communist states in Asia and Eastern Europe have transformed and are setting new benchmarks in development. They have raised the bar that had been set far too low by failed Asian and African states in the last 60 years. This is a singularly good thing to happen to the entire developing world. It brings us even closer to the reckoning that India ought to change. However, despite its size and diversity, it is still a stable nation. Therefore, it is important not to make any drastic revolutionary changes and maybe to chart a stepwise evolutionary path, learning as we go.

INDIA—A WAY FORWARD

Legislating the Flaws Away—Minimal Essential Changes

Several of the changes recommended for democracy are relevant to India as well. As has been said for other nations, there are few checks on the political parties. They are free to use any means howsoever rudimentary, manipulative or divisive, to come to power. There is a need to curb and ban the use of sectarian divisive tactics like caste, language, religion, or region in campaigns, as well as media reporting of results along these dimensions. While hard to implement, this endeavor is important such that democracy focuses more on governance issues rather than manipulating the electorate along divisive dimensions.

The second change requires strengthening of the federal government in line with its constitution. In Indian elections, slowly the national mandate has got fragmented and regional parties have come to dominate the federal elections as well. The coalitions that result pull the government in myriad different directions leading to do-nothing-ism. Germany's system of a minimum 5% of national vote cut off for representation in the national parliament could be instituted. Nations like Poland and Romania have already increased stability by instituting this mechanism. It is indeed already followed by most European democracies. Further, a "positive vote of confidence" should be required to bring down a government, thus preventing smaller partners from playing kingmakers. These changes may require a move to the PR method of vote counting. This would go some way in clearing the parliamentary cobwebs that have choked Indian political decision making. If brought about, these changes would help the national government perform the role it is supposedly mandated by the constitution) which in the last two decades has been weakened considerably at the hands of a splintered mandate).

Ideally what India needs is a unity government akin to Colombia's National Front or Spain's *turno pacific*, which catapulted those nations to a much higher level of development. But given India's size and stability, such a drastic change in its political set up would prove too risky. A pragmatic transitional alternative could be a grand coalition between its two large national level parties, Congress and the BJP. This should be preceded by a "positive vote of confidence" legislative change, else the coalition may not be stable. Such grand coalitions have existed in many developed world democracies. Germany had a grand coalition between the SDP and the CDU/CSU during 2005–2009. In Austria, a grand coalition existed between its two large parties, the People's Party and the Social Democratic Party, for long periods, first during the crucial post World War II era in 1945–1966 and then again between 1986–2000. The first coalition helped Austria redevelop its war ravaged economy and the second one too proved stable and progressive.

If India's two large parties (that have of late converged in their development goals for the nation) could bring about a similar grand coalition, they would give India the long term development focus it so badly needs. In the 2009 elections, the two parties have won an almost equal vote share and in any case India is long used to anti incumbency voting so rarely does a party win two successive terms, even though Congress led UPA has in the 2009 elections. If a grand coalition could be as stable as it was in Austria and could last for a period of 20 years or so, it would allow India to undertake long stalled investment projects. India may also be able to modernize its agricultural system and avert its looming water scarcity crisis. Even the development agenda could be pursued in a focused manner to create genuine employment rather than the wasteful or amenable to corruption freebie schemes that are being run. However this would require a natural convergence between the leadership of the two national parties as well as their commitment to making the grand coalition work. But if that is brought about, it would allow the strengths of India's democratic setup to be sustained without crippling its development. There is a need to anchor India's democracy, and the future rests with its leadership. Further, in some of the truly backward states like Bihar, where the leadership is progressive, a unity single party state government could be tried—provided the political rivals agree to it. That could help them curb their poverty and violence since decades of democracy has yielded negligible returns in these specific instances.

When we look at the developed nations, they metamorphosed into their present state from largely poor rural ones through a different mechanism. They instituted parliamentary forms of government but kept the voting rights limited to a property-owning minority and extended it cautiously and gradually over a century or two. Such oligarch republics were far superior to a grand coalition (if feasible) or a unitary party rule that is being recommended for most developing world nations. In essence it was a better system as it centralized the power and authority yet allowed freedom of expression as well as checks on the government. However, much has changed as most of the democratic world has already seen universal suffrage. Going back to limited suffrage can incite social revolt and hence is ruled out as an option for the developing world of today, even though it is a better checked system than a unitary party rule. But universal suffrage democracy thus far has disabled development and thus transient unitary models are necessitated. As the nations near a developed status, slowly more open political systems can be tried; but in the present state, they are counter-productive.

Talking about change, it would be wise to look at two examples, Russia and China, to highlight best practices as well as mistakes to avoid in the process. There are also many important lessons therein for rest of the developing world.

USSR TO RUSSIA—THE TUMULTUOUS JOURNEY

In the mid 1980s, Mikhail Gorbachev initiated the much needed political and economic opening up in the USSR. But it led to unpredictable consequences and nearly destroyed the nation. What went wrong and how did the nation pull itself back together again?

To start with, what were Gorbachev's credentials for leading the change? In the Soviet era, Gorbachev had a stellar career. Academically bright since childhood, he went on to achieve many successes ahead of his time. At the age of just 16, he was awarded the Order of the Red Banner of Labor for his efforts in collective farming. In 1970, he became one of the youngest provincial party chiefs in the USSR. His positions in the CPSU created opportunities for him to travel abroad. These shaped his early ideas for a need for change within the communist USSR. Internationally he was well received and credited with having a sharp and open mind. In 1975, he led a delegation to Germany, in 1983 to Canada and in 1984 to the UK. Based on an in depth study of the Western political and economic model, Gorbachev crafted a plan of comprehensive reforms within the USSR. He initiated two landmark policy programs, Glasnost (denoting political openness and transparency) and Perestroika (denoting economic liberalization and political reforms). At the time, the Western world too advocated a quick dismantling of the Soviet economy to make way for free market reforms.

However, once these studied policies were implemented, the results were markedly different from what was intended or expected. In all elections, regional nationalists swept the mandate across the Soviet republics and started demanding autonomy and independence. Ethnic tensions started simmering throughout the region wherever communal differences existed. Economically, it was a worse disaster. Massive tax evasions occurred, eroding the base of the federal government. As the old power structure got dismantled, the republics as well as the local governments refused to pay taxes to the central government. State employees thus could not be paid wages and were often paid in barter goods for their work. Coal miners were particularly hard hit by this. The elimination of central control over production decisions led to a breakdown of the supply chain and extreme shortages accrued of essential goods and commodities. Spurious banks mushroomed without any regulations and collapsed shortly, sinking investors' money with them. Inflation skyrocketed. The "shock therapy"[1] advocated by Western institutions led to quick privatization of state-owned enterprises. The communist era party bosses usurped all the gains and turned into oligarchs. Racket gangs sprang up everywhere to exploit the black economy and loot the newly opened national resources. None of the revolutionary objectives were achieved.

---

1 Shock Therapy — Dismantling Communism, Russian Economic Reform in the 1990s, History of Post Soviet Russia, Spiritus-Temporis.com, http://www.spiritus-temporis.com/history-of-post-soviet-russia/dismantling-communism.html

By mid 1990s, Russia sank into a deep economic depression accompanied by a breakdown of law and order in the society as well as political instability in all its provinces. The constituent republics had already broken off and declared independence. Smaller and manageable in size, they were doing much better than Mother Russia. Even in the late Soviet era, while overall prosperity was not high, poverty as estimated by World Bank affected only 1.5% of the population. By 1993, this had risen to 39–49% of the population. Life expectancy dropped sharply, especially among males, due to diseases as well as other unnatural causes like murder, suicide and accidents. Alcoholism as well as related deaths rose sharply.

On the eve of an emerging bankruptcy, however, arose a leader that once again proved the Russian grit. Reviled the world over, loved in his home state, Vladimir Putin provided one of the factors that often determines the future of nations undergoing war or crisis—leadership. He emerged from within the system, first appointed by Boris Yeltsin as his successor and then winning the 2000 election. Putin led Russia out of the dark tunnel during his two terms. Political and ethnic insurgency was dealt with strongly, though that invited widespread international criticism. Law and order was restored internally, thus setting the stage ready for economic recovery. This was followed by a focus on industrialization, streamlining of the oil industry and wooing foreign investment. As a result, GDP started growing at about 7% p.a., soon making Russia the 6th largest economy in the world. Population below poverty line came down to about 14% in 2007 and unemployment to 6%. Achieving an HDI of 0.817, Russia has broken into the higher developed nations category.[1] All of Putin's measures could not be termed democratic, especially in terms of dealing with insurgents, and press freedom also remains limited in Russia. But to pull the nation out of the crisis, such measures were necessary.

This was understood by earlier Western philosophers who also lived in societies undergoing sharp upheavals. For instance, Edmund Burke wrote "Reflections on the Revolution in France" in 1790 at the beginning of the revolution, severely criticizing it. He focused on practicality of solutions instead of abstract ideas. "What is the use of discussing a man's abstract right to food or to medicine? The question is upon method of procuring and ad-

---

1 "Russia's Economy Stabilized Under Putin," Jim Heintz, 1 Mar 2008, *USA Today*, http://www.usatoday.com/news/world/2008-03-01-2880654134_x.htm

ministering them."[1] In his view, a political doctrine founded on abstractions such as liberty and the rights of man could just as easily be abused and turn tyrannical. This is exactly the kind of thinking Putin followed—instead of theorizing, he went about putting the administration in order.

Let us assess the procedural changes during Putin's regime as well as the character of the economy that was created during this era. Legal reforms were a landmark achievement of his first term. He succeeded in codifying land laws and tax laws which had long been stalled by oligarchic power blocs. Other legal reforms included new codes on labor and administrative, criminal, commercial and civil procedural laws as well as major statutes on bar. In order to bring tax evasion under control, a simpler, more streamlined tax code was adopted in 2001 introducing a flat 13% tax rate; this reduced the tax burden on people yet dramatically increased state revenue through effective implementation.[2] In 2004, Putin signed the Kyoto protocol treaty designed to reduce greenhouse gases that bigger developed nations were yet to ratify. Most nations round the world are running deficit budgets and allowing debt to balloon. Under Putin, the Russian federal budget ran surpluses every year, reaching about 6% of the GDP in 2007. Unlike the Middle Eastern economies, Russia diversified its industry and many sectors of the economy were developed. (However, it still ranks high on the corruption perception index and many social problems remain.) Putin's public approval ratings have surpassed those of any leader in the world today reaching about 84% in 2007.

While Russia has bounced back, the lost decades could perhaps have been avoided if Russia had not opened up suddenly and violently. As Putin himself has summed up, the revolutionary manner of Soviet dismantlement was "a national tragedy on an enormous scale" from which only the existing elites and nationalists of the Republics gained. The ordinary citizens lost considerably.

No doubt Soviet Russia had to change but the pace and manner of it was wrong. We can say that with the benefit of hindsight now. Nations like Myanmar or Iraq, which have been pushed into or are being pushed into a violent overthrow of old systems and structures, have gone through

---

1 Edmund Burke, Reflections on the Revolution in France, Liberty, Equality, Fraternity, Exploring the French Revolution, http://chnm.gmu.edu/revolution/d/563/

2 Putin's Economy — Eight Years on, Katya Malofeeva and Tim Brenton, Renaissance Capital, 15 Aug 2007, Russia Profile.org, http://www.russiaprofile.org/page.php?pageid=Business&articleid=a1187177738

and will go through similar disasters. There is no guarantee that there will be a Putin to rescue them, however. In contrast, let us look at change as it was handled in China.

CHINA—THE LAST WORD

Defying all conventional wisdom and "international expert opinion," doggedly and diligently China has crafted a path of its own. And maybe if we are honest enough to admit it, it has blazed a trail for others to follow. As per the World Bank, between 1981 and 2005, the world poverty rate fell by about 25%. China accounted for most of the improvement, as its population living in poverty fell from 85% to just 15.9%. Roughly 600 million people were delivered from abject poverty[1] defined as $1.25 per day. This level of accelerated development and poverty reduction is unprecedented in human history. The nation has already been recognized for its achievements, its model studied and the lessons are widely known. Yet let us review them briefly.

The Chinese media often expresses embarrassment that the country has produced a great economy but hardly any economists. The irony of that statement perhaps escapes them but therein lies China's success. Instead of chasing abstract ideas about the "rights of man," China set about finding the best possible methods of "procuring them." Deng Xiaoping, considered the father of Chinese modernization reforms, said one must seek truth from facts. The key feature of this model was pragmatism,[2] driven less by an ideology and more by the process of experimenting through trial and error. Policies were crafted, tested on a small scale, studied for their consequences, and if proven effective, were implemented at a fast rate in other areas.

China's pioneering concept of socio-economic zones, SEZs, was one such idea. Instead of liberalizing the whole nation, a small zone was cordoned off for economic liberalization. It was immensely successful and it helped China learn the dynamics of a market economy. The success was then easy to replicate across the nation. Likewise state controlled pricing

---

1 "World Bank's Poverty Estimates Revised," Anup Shah, Aug 2008, *Global Issues*, http://www.globalissues.org/article/4/poverty-around-the-world#WorldBanksPovertyEstimatesRevised

2 " 'China Model' Result of Determined Leadership," Stanley Crossick, 24 Mar 2010, *Global Times*, http://crossick.blogactiv.eu/2010/03/24/china-model-result-of-determined-leadership/

---

was phased out gradually, first replaced by dual pricing in farms as well as factories and slowly changed to full market pricing. The gradual changes helped the nation make corrections along the way as well as learn to operate under new economic principles. In 1990 the state sector accounted for 70% of the output in China. Through sustained initiatives and growth of private industry, this declined to 40% by 2002 and continues declining. While the economy was liberalized, the political authority remained unchanged with the Communist Party of China. However, party mechanisms were introduced with periodic rotation of leadership positions. Further going against the tide of pure market economy, China chose to make huge public investment in infrastructure. This one decision proved crucial to China's exponential growth. As a result China has been the fastest growing major economy in the world, averaging about 10% p.a.

The positive role between public infrastructure investment and economic growth has been studied even in the developed world. As per Shuanglin Lin's research,[1] Ashauer (1989) argued that the slowdown of US productivity was related to the decrease in public infrastructure investment. Munnell (1990) showed how states that have invested in infrastructure tend to have greater output, more private investment, and higher employment growth. Canning, Fay, and Perotti (1994) found "substantial effects of physical infrastructure on economic growth based on the international data set." It has been noted that relying on the private sector to develop infrastructure, especially in poor countries, has not been effective. Infrastructure projects have a long lifecycle in terms of rate of return whereas the investment required upfront is huge. Short to medium term oriented stock markets do not reward such initiatives. Private provisions also tend to prevent the poor from getting needed infrastructure services. Public Investments in infrastructure and education have proven to be the long term income redistributive mechanism. Infrastructure creation also has lifestyle benefits for the average citizen. Unlike most developing nations, China rarely has power outages, public transportation is inexpensive, and water supply is streamlined.

There are some trends to China's poverty reduction. As the reforms started, just switching to dual pricing and related moves led to economic growth; and poverty was reduced considerably in the early 1980s. This was

---

1 Public Infrastructure Development in China, Lin Shuanglin, 22 Jun 2001, Comparative Economic Studies, http://www.highbeam.com/doc/1G1-78479862.html

just picking the low hanging fruits produced by the change from a state-controlled economy to a market economy, as noted by Martin Ravallion of the World Bank.[1] This was followed by a decade of stagnation, from the mid 1980s to the early 1990s, which was really the investment phase in China. The nation upgraded its infrastructure, roads, power supply, ports, and airports, and also invested in higher education. Within 10–15 years this started paying off as the poverty rate started declining again. However, these reforms that China embraced were opposed by the people initially, and many large protests occurred during the 1980s where people expressed dissatisfaction with China's ruling party. The reforms that the party had initiated remained unpopular as people had not "yet" seen any perceptible benefits. But as prosperity started spreading, this view changed dramatically.

The 2000s were the dawn of a new era in China as all its reforms and investments of the previous two decades started bearing fruit; the economy boomed. There are lessons here for the developing world, and they show why democracy cannot work. It appears that there is a long investment phase of about 10–15 years in a poor, dilapidated state before the benefits are experienced by the population at large. No democratic government can convince its electorate to wait that long. The latter will almost certainly sabotage the investment phase. Activists and opinion leaders will help them along, calling the government pro-rich, as no real perceptible benefits can be seen. This sabotaging of the investment phase has been going on in India for quite some time now. That is why poverty remains as high as it is.

In 1978, 71% of the labor force in China was employed in agriculture. The quota-based communes were dismantled, allowing individuals to sell part of the produce in the market. At the same time, the population was encouraged to move to other avenues such as the industrial sector. The government invested in irrigation projects like the Three Gorges Dam, introduced modern farming methods, and also later started operating large state farms. Today only 23% the population is employed in agriculture, yet farm productivity is high and China has become one of the leading producers and exporters of food. According to the UN, China fed 20% of the world's population with only 7% of the world's arable land. China has limited arable land—137.1 million hectares as compared to India's 160.5 million hectares.

---

1 *Fighting Poverty: Findings and Lessons from China's Success*, Martin Ravallion and Shaohua Chen, Research at the World Bank, http://econ.worldbank.org/WBSITE/EXTERNAL/EXTDEC/EXTRESEARCH/0,,contentMDK:20634060-pagePK:641654 01-piPK:64165026-theSitePK:469382,00.html

China ranks first worldwide in terms of farm output. This once again shows the importance of greater farm productivity using better technology, larger farms and a smaller percentage of the population employed in agriculture.

Overall, China enforced development through its centralized, controlled political structure. It has a large public healthcare system and regularly invests over 6% of the GDP in education. The communists had always supported women's emancipation and through education and legal reforms, a certain amount of equality was achieved. With growing opportunities as well as modern education, gender discrimination that has been a problem in China has naturally come down in the urban areas. This further helped promotion of the one-child policy. Today, women enjoy a great degree of freedom in terms of access to education, employment and general safety. China has responded to large scale natural calamities like earthquakes in a manner hailed as exemplary in the developing world. Economically, it still relies on its natural abundant coal as an energy source, much like Europe in the 19th century. As it edges towards a developed status, it must address higher order issues and start making concerted efforts at environmental protection. Challenges remain before this economy as it is export dependent; and with rising living standards and labor costs, it may face competition from other lower cost economies. But most developing economies in Asia and Africa are still unstable and caught in their democratic web of opposition and deliberations, so this threat becomes real only if the others get their political act together.

China has just moved out of large scale abject poverty. Its per capita income, in purchasing power parity terms, is still just $6,567 as compared to developed nations like the US with $46,381, the UK at $34,619 or Germany at $34,212. But with a focused and expedient government in place, China is developing at an unprecedented pace and perhaps it will be comparable to the developed world in 20 years' time. As of now, it lacks a stable, strong middle class, and any move to bring in democratic reforms, which the CCP is not considering anyway, could reverse its path to progress. However, once it is more developed, internally it may face pressures for greater freedom of expression, which in any case is required to move up the economic value chain. But that time is still many years away. One of China's key strengths is disciplined leadership which has evolved into a genuine party mechanism with rotation of top leadership every 8 years; this has helped keep out any cult of particular leaders. If this balance continues, China may continue to grow.

As the Russian example shows, even the most carefully studied policies can backfire, especially in large, diverse nations. Yet change should not be avoided if it is necessary. Perhaps if handled in small, step-wise, measured doses as was done in China, the risks associated with change come down substantially.

Moving on from a comparative analysis of the mechanisms of change, let us now sum up the results of democracy in the developing world, taking all aspects discussed thus far into account.

SUMMING UP

The idea of a representative democratic republic was invented to bring in a checked form of government that respected the rule of law, freedom, and civil rights, and worked for the greater good of the society. This did not happen in the developing world as universal suffrage democracy was implemented in nation after nation. One of the key reasons is that poverty is hard to break out of. It takes nations decades, if not longer, of concerted effort to pull people out of abject poverty in a perceptible manner. Yet elections have to be won every 4–5 years. Not having a credible story to relate to the electorate, increasingly democracy politics revolves around distribution of freebies or bribes as well as hijacking votes through emotional, divisive issues. A general rise in crime as well as public support for radical and often violent ideologies are all too common phenomena as a result of premature political opening up. Thus, in most nations democracy itself does not bring stability. Even in the few where it has stabilized the society, it has not met the development objectives. It may be time to challenge our perfect theory—democracy may not be the answer to the developing world's problems.

At a broader level, the 20th century has been a landmark with great scientific and technological advances on one hand but also an unprecedented population explosion on the other. The world population was just 978 million in the year 1800, and only went up to 1.6 billion in the year 1900. However, this galloped to 6 billion by the year 2000, a whopping 375% increase. Most of this has been added at the lower (poor) end, primarily in the developing world. The resultant increase in widespread poverty and destitution has become a grave problem. By turning to market reforms, most nations have seen slight improvements in the last two decades, but the development process is often stalled due to people's initial resistance and mistrust of it. Given the size of the problem, it cannot be tackled through charitable initiatives or "give something free" pro-poor programs. The solutions will have to be systemic through better suited political and economic models.

Based on existing evidence, transient models could be evolved for various nations. One of the formulae that seem to have worked in some nations that have broken out of the poverty mode is to couple centralized politics with decentralized economics. Centralized politics in the form of party rule with rotation of leadership as well as participative party mechanisms (as was done under KANU in Kenya or under the CCP in China) have been successful. But such experiences are limited and while democracy seems detrimental in the developing world, what works is not as well understood. In that case it becomes imperative to follow evolutionary change through small measured steps with constant assessment and validation of policies.

Instead of a one-solution-fits-all approach, strategies ought to be tailor-made to suit the varying needs of vastly different nations while also taking their present power dynamic and key stakeholders into account. For unstable democracies, a turn to a more centralized structured unity or single party rule may provide a way forward. The stable democracies on the other hand may slowly evolve hybrid mechanisms that help them address their pressing problems. But their path would be the most complex to navigate as stability during change ought to remain their first priority.

As we learn from experiences of more successes in the developing world, new political theories could be formulated around that evidence, but theories ought not to be propagated in a vacuum, ignoring evidence on the ground. As reaffirmed through the discussions, democracy does remain an ideal long term goal. But perhaps the road to it is not as quick, easy and simple as it has, so far, been assumed to be.

CHAPTER 10. THE DECREE: WHAT IS GOOD GOVERNANCE?

Democracy no doubt has achieved much in the Western world. As is the case with any system tried, problems abound there, too, but essentially the system does work. In its progressive form, where basic elements like habeas corpus, rule of law, presence of political and civil liberties, separation of religion and state as well as separation of powers, etc., have been established and the political power rests with a prosperous and progressive middle class, the system has many strengths. The process to get there is a long and arduous one, and even after reaching there, efforts, thoughts and initiatives are required to keep the system progressive. It is a hard to achieve end. The mechanistic juxtaposition of elections and a formal constitution alone, as so many nations in the developing world have tried, does not create a progressive democracy. That is the reason more centralized political systems and unitary state models, despite their attendant weaknesses, have been proposed for the developing nations. But as these nations become developed, democracy should ideally and hopefully be their future as well.

But, even if democracy may not be the instant and right alternative for the developing world, the acceptable alternatives are still not dictatorial authoritarian rules. How do we assess a system which does not derive its inherent right to rule from being an elected government? As we create and balance different systems in the world, in line with their vastly different governance needs, there are some common ways to assess the alternate systems, which remains focused on the "for the people" dimension of governance. Millennia ago, Aristotle defined this in simple terms—a state that exists for the ruled as benevolent and for the ruler as despotic. We need to define in concrete terms what that should translate into.

DEFINING THE "END"—MEASURES OF GOOD GOVERNANCE

"A perfection of means, and confusion of aims, seems to be our main problem." Albert Einstein's words seem to define the crux of our political problem quite aptly. What we measure is what we get. So far, our predominant focus has been on measuring democracy or its processes, not really the end governance. This confusion of means, which democracy all but is, with the ends, which ideally "good governance as delivered" should be, is the source of many problems.

The United Nations defines good governance[1] in terms of eight major characteristics—participation, transparency, consensus orientation, equity and inclusiveness, rule of law, effectiveness & efficiency and accountability. The definition is quite clearly focused on "the means" or the processes and seems like a force fit to democracy. If all we measure is processes, such as free elections or participation, then that is all we are going to get. A nation like Ghana has done just that. Diligently and sincerely it has worked for years to establish each of the above processes, and to its credit has achieved considerable success. However, that has not translated into development or a better livelihood for its people. It certainly has most of the elements of good governance as defined above, but it lags far behind nations which have almost none of the above. These processes of democracy do not automatically lead to good governance. Likewise South Africa has "participation" and "rule of law" but that does not lead to an orderly society. The majority simply gets hijacked by regressive societal values and practices. Yet its regime is accorded more legitimacy, because it is elected, than some who are delivering far better governance but are "not elected" like, say, Tanzania or Rwanda.

The digital definition of good governance as either having or not having a democracy is misleading. Some democratic governments have delivered poor governance whereas some non-democratic ones have delivered good

---

1 What is Good Governance? 2010, United Nations ESCAP, http://www.unescap. org/pdd/prs/ProjectActivities/Ongoing/gg/governance.asp

governance to their citizens. Even among the developed world democracies, nations vary considerably on how well governed they are. What needs to be recognized is the "delivered to citizens" part. Elections are just a means of forming the government; the government then needs to be assessed not just on what processes it is following but what is the net outcome for the citizens in their day-to-day lives. The presence of mechanistic democracy but absence of good governance is evident in people's widespread disillusionment with their respective governments and leaders. If we were to define end governance in terms of deliverables, they would translate into criteria like the following:

Widespread prosperity. The first dimension of good governance should clearly be based on the economic progress the nation is making for its citizens. This would be based on objective criteria like average per capita income, quotient of income inequality, and population below poverty line. Over the years, trends should be assessed to see the direction of the citizens' economic well being. For instance, Nigeria and Cameroon have similar per capita income at $2,150 and $2,227 respectively. But their population below the poverty line (less than $1.25 a day) is vastly different with 64.4% for Nigeria and 32.8% for Cameroon. Regardless of criteria like "consensus orientation," Cameroon seems to be delivering relatively better on this critical economic dimension of governance. The trends over time reveal the direction each country is headed.

Good Law and Order. This is a crucial dimension in determining an average citizen's daily quality of life. The overall social and political environment should be stable and sustainable. People should be free to live and exist without undue worry about violence and crime, whether perpetrated by state or non state factors. There should be no persecution of minorities and they should enjoy equal rights. Violence against women and children particularly should be controlled. A nation like South Africa may have participation and consensus as well as rule of law, but if it is the crime capital of the world, it remains poorly governed. Governments must derive their legitimacy based on how well governed they are rather than simply whether or not they have won an election.

Rule of Law. This remains an important dimension of any progressive rule. While democracy may not be a viable model immediately, a reversal to arbitrary dictatorships could be worse. A nation ought to be ruled as per law and everyone ought to be equal before law. The writ of habeas corpus and lawful trial of offenders ought to be in place and adjudged for its implementation in reality.

Access to basic public amenities. Do people have access to clean fresh drinking water, medical care, roads, electricity, means of transport, toilets, drainage, footpaths, public open space, etc.? In India, for instance, since the market reforms of 1991, the average per capita income has gone up but all public amenities have deteriorated. The key reason is lack of investment in infrastructure. So this measure is distinct from a simple measure of prosperity.

Education. In the developing world, literacy rates remain low for a large number of nations. Investment in education tends to yield returns in the medium to long term but many a democracy forsakes these objectives in preference for short term measures. In the developed world, too, some nations like Sweden invested heavily in education and skills training in the late 1990s but the voters did not reward them. So the mere presence of democracy, once again, does not ensure the population will get educated. Yet these are the criteria that determine the future direction of a nation. It may be achieved through public or private means. Highlighting different governments' achievements in education may help the electorate take sharper notice of it. Although this dimension is already a part of the Human Development Index and nations are measured on that, somehow when we assess different nations, we ignore HDI and simply focus on whether or not they have a democracy.

Degree of Freedom. How well are people's basic as well as higher order freedom needs met and what is the direction? If a state is relatively crime free, poverty free and allows freedom of expression as well as press freedom, it could be recognized as truly free.

Financial Astuteness and Efficiency. Balancing a budget is an important governance deliverable. Many times when governments undertake this exercise, voters do not reward them. On the other hand, some governments dole out benefits and run huge deficits year on year. That is appealing to voters in the short run, even though it turns the economy inflationary or debt dependent, as has now happened in most nations round the world. If we were measuring governments on such specific criteria, the problems would be highlighted before they became a crisis. If such governance deliverables are defined, measured and highlighted, perhaps they could even help improve voters' discretion.

Harmonious Foreign Policy. It is important for nations to not just be well governed internally, but they should also pursue a foreign policy that adds to the world rather than subtract from it. Nations that contribute humanitarian aid or mediate in conflict resolution should be credited with good governance on this measure. For instance India pursues a harmonious foreign policy and even gives protection to political exiles, yet without ever inciting trouble or insurgency in neighboring nations. Conversely, nations that export terror, engage in hateful rhetoric or unjust wars lack in good governance on this dimension. Such dimensions must get their due credit, or debit, as the case may be.

Contribution to Human Advancement. This is a higher order governance deliverable, perhaps expected more of the developed nations. But it highlights the long term perspective and why democracy is needed in the long run. This dimension of governance means contribution to science and technology, innovations, literature, and art. That is something to be highlighted as "great" governance must enable an environment conducive to greater cultural, literary, and scientific advancements.

Care for Environment. This should include criteria like measuring the percentage of energy consumption met through clean sources and measuring the level of pollution. This should also include conservation of natural resources like water. Environment protection and conservation are equally essential for developing nations and developed ones. For instance, the depletion of the water table has led to catastrophic problems in Africa; it could lead some Asian nations and the Middle East to a crisis as well; and even the Great Plains of the United States are under strain.

The focus should be on criteria that are concrete, measurable and draw a balance between short and long term needs of a nation. More importantly, these criteria measure what is finally delivered to citizens rather than mere processes of governance. This is not to say that objectives like participation and consensus orientation are not important—but those are hard to measure and there is no guarantee that they will result in better governance. For instance in a poor, elementary society, participation may sometimes drive it towards fundamentalism. Likewise, governance through consensus orientation can be taken to an extreme, as in coalition governments which result in do-nothing-ism, which is the opposite of good governance.

Processes are important in their own right, and we should keep assessing and reviewing them. But in measuring what is good governance, we should measure end results, not supposed processes. It is time to stop projecting democracy as the means, the ends, and everything in between. Democracies themselves vary greatly in different nations, and if measured on end deliverables to citizens, may fail on several of the above criteria. This should help knock the complacency out of them. If, on the other hand, some other systems are delivering good governance, that should and would be highlighted if we were to measure nations on governance rather than merely on "democracy". Governments should derive their legitimacy not on the basis of how they were formed but how well they govern in reality. Our prime allegiance should be to ends and not means.

If we start measuring nations on these end deliverables, to our surprise, we may start getting them. If even half of these governance deliverables are achieved in the developing world, it would indeed make for a bright future.

> When we blindly adopt a religion, a political system, a literary dogma, we become automatons. We cease to grow.
>
> —Anaïs Nin (French author, 1903–1977)

ADDITIONAL SOURCE NOTES

The following sources were invaluable in researching the book and were used for all countries studied initially (about 150 nations with a population of at least a million).

BBC Country Profiles – for recent political history, http://news.bbc.co.uk/2/hi/country_profiles/default.stm

The World Bank, Countries and Regions – topical issues facing different countries and regions, http://web.worldbank.org/WBSITE/EXTERNAL/COUNTRIES/0„pagePK:180619-theSitePK:136917,00.html

United Nations Development Programme (UNDP) – Human Development Reports, http://hdr.undp.org/en/, http://www.undp.org/

CIA The World Factbook – primary source of data on demographics, government structure and Economic profile of countries https://www.cia.gov/library/publications/the-world-factbook/

Countries of the World, infoplease.com – a secondary compilation offering interactive trend analysis especially on information dating back to the 1960s and onwards, http://www.infoplease.com/countries.html#axzz0zwEmqKza

Students of the World, another secondary compilation of information on countries of the world. http://www.studentsoftheworld.info/menu_infopays.html

History of Nations.net – timelines and key events, a cross reference, http://www.historyofnations.net/

The Internet Classics Archive – for political philosophical works from ancient times, © 1994-2009, Daniel C. Stevenson, Web Atomics, http://classics.mit.edu/

AUTHOR'S NOTE

This book started almost 12 years back when I met Lee, a student from Singapore, at the University of Kentucky. We had a heated debate about democracy where I spoke for it and he against it. The argument remained inconclusive, but up until that point I had always considered democracy to be "a given." It opened a window in my mind and I started viewing the unfolding world events from a new perspective where the superiority of democracy was no longer assumed. This led me to start researching and writing this book in earnestness about five years back.

Born and brought up in India, I have lived in all four of its main regions. I worked in Marketing and Marketing Research, which allowed me to travel extensively throughout the country, including rural parts of many states like Orissa, UP and Maharashtra. In my younger days, I lived in Botswana for a brief period and was amazed at the pleasant, easy going and "non aggressive" culture compared to the prevalent prejudices. I also met a set of friends from Zaire (now Democratic Republic of Congo) who were enjoying a quiet, peaceful existence there. It shocked me all the more when that peace was destroyed later. I have had the fortune of traveling to many countries in the world. For the last three years, I have been living in China and enjoying life as an ordinary citizen.

The book is written from a bottom-up perspective, from the viewpoint of a citizen—showing what the alternate political models deliver in reality. Although it is based on scientific research and not anecdotal personal experiences, I believe that living in a country brings a reality check that enriches pure academic analysis.

I studied science, education and management from Delhi University. Not being a political science or history student helped me stay open to perspectives outside those being taught. Perhaps it takes a non indoctrinated person sometimes to take a clear view of the "Emperor's new clothes." At the same time, researching and writing this book helped me change many of my beliefs and assumptions, and I hope it helps change some for the readers too.

I would like to thank some of my friends and family who have helped and supported me—Neelima, for being my key motivator and biggest supporter, and my late father who had the maximum influence on my thinking, education and beliefs. I thank Ramesh for his general help and support and also Pratibha for being my friend in need. I would also like to thank countless people and avatars I met online, from a wide range of nationalities and backgrounds, who helped shape many of my ideas and thinking style.

I thank Algora Publishing for giving me a platform and for their excellent resources and guidelines for new authors. Their counsel, "Don't give opinions, prove it," particularly helped me evolve as a researcher, and Martin DeMers' direction and guidance helped give the book the right structure and form, true to its aim.